7
SECRETS
to
POWER
PRAYING

HOW *to* ACCESS GOD'S WISDOM
and MIRACLES EVERY DAY

JANE GLENCHUR

Chosen

a division of Baker Publishing Group
Minneapolis, Minnesota

© 2014 by Jane Glenchur

Published by Chosen Books
11400 Hampshire Avenue South
Bloomington, Minnesota 55438
www.chosenbooks.com

Chosen Books is a division of
Baker Publishing Group, Grand Rapids, Michigan

Printed in the United States of America

Library of Congress Cataloging-in-Publication Data
Glenchur, Jane.
    7 secrets to power praying : how to access God's Wisdom and miracles every day / Jane Glenchur ; Randy Clark.
        pages   cm.
    Includes bibliographical references.
    Summary: "Learn how to receive extraordinary answers to everyday prayers! Access God's wisdom for life's decisions—big and small—with step-by-step guidance and pratical tips"—provided by the publisher.
    ISBN 978-0-8007-9571-9 (pbk. : alk. paper)
    1. Prayer—Christianity. I. Title. II. Title: Seven secrets to power praying.
BV210.3.G57 2014
248.3'2—dc23   2013039303

Some names and details in this book have been changed to preserve privacy.

The information given in 7 Secrets to Power Praying is biblical and spiritual in nature. It is not medical counsel and should not be viewed as such. Jane Glenchur, Chosen Books and Baker Publishing Group hereby disclaim any and all responsibility or liability for any adverse or damaging effects that may be asserted or claimed to have arisen as a result of use of this material.

Cover design by Dual Identity, Inc.

Author is represented by Leslie H. Stobbe

14   15   16   17   18   19   20   7   6   5   4   3   2

I lovingly dedicate this book to my mother,
Elizabeth Belz,
who taught me to persevere. No matter how
strong the wind or how high the waves, you
showed me how to stay the course.

Contents

Contents

Foreword

I have known Jane Glenchur, M.D., for several years. Her new book, *7 Secrets to Power Praying: How to Access God's Wisdom and Miracles Every Day*, is a wonderful book full of practical insights into the nature of God and prayer. Jane's personal story from M.D. to M.O.M. while her husband is out of work is the beginning of her new walk of faith. I believe she brings to us a wealth of information that is both practical and powerful. Jane begins by addressing the resistance many believers have to including God in the smallest decisions of their lives. She deals with the cessationist view of God as One who does not communicate and why this is an unbiblical picture of God. Jane believes God likes to communicate with us, and she is determined to help us discover how to have such dialogue with Him—prayer.

Jane helps us to see that we do not have to be *super-saints* to be heard by God. Jane lays out for us the things that please God, the things that move God to release heavenly answers to earthly problems. She does this by pointing out the importance of five keys to answered prayers: petition, passion, presence, preparedness and perseverance.

Jane addresses our skeptical mindsets and our small world-view of God. She asks if we go to Google or to God for our answers. She cautions us not to allow our brains to limit the unlimited wisdom of God. In her third chapter she deals with the role common sense plays, including what Scripture tells us about logic and reasoning, pointing out that the hotline to heaven is connected to the right brain. Jane encourages us and shows us how to make the switch from predominant dependence upon left-brain thinking to trusting in faith from the right brain.

Jane has written about seven secrets to more abundant living: (#1) Say Yes First; (#2) Give God Your Password; (#3) Tap into God's Heart; (#4) Toss the Pros and Cons List; (#5) Know When to Give Up; (#6) Open Locked Doors; and (#7) Employ the Power of Testimonies.

There is also much more to the book than these seven secrets of prayer. It is packed full of practical, helpful teaching and instruction on how to live a more abundant life by staying connected to God. Jane teaches us about the absolute power of learning how to say yes to God, pointing out that our inability to say yes is rooted in hidden doubts, unbelief and fear. She raises the questions, What does yes actually mean spiritually? What do we do if we cannot say yes to God?

Jane writes from the experience of a mother as well as a doctor. Her chapter "Give God Your Password" is a favorite of mine. This chapter teaches how to turn miserable circumstances into miraculous blessings. Readers will discover how to preempt bad moods and keep connected to the messages from heaven.

Jane indicates that instead of prayer being a laundry list of requests, it should be a time of engaging God. Information gained through communion with Him is the way to obtain direction for a satisfying, meaningful future. This leadership from God is better and wiser than our pros and cons lists. Jane invites us into a relationship with God where even when we face locked doors, when we are outwitted and outnumbered by our obstacles, when our circumstances are insurmountable, God is still able to bring us into victory. Learn how to let God open doors of opportunity for you. Jane admonishes her readers not to miss out on their miracles because they quit too soon. In this chapter she teaches how the application of John 3:8 can reverse impossibilities and turn them into successes.

Jane shows how sharing your story of what God is doing in your life multiplies the blessing, increasing God's fruit in our lives. She helps readers learn how to give their stories.

Jane draws the book to its final chapters by focusing on very down-to-earth teaching on the specifics of making prayer requests, how to block interference from the enemy and what to do if you are met with silence. It gives a detailed discussion on the importance of confirming the directives you receive and how to obtain those confirmations. Once again she illustrates with Scripture and personal stories.

One of my favorite chapters is "Unmasking Deception." Jane asks, How do we discern deception from God's truth? How do we confirm whether we are hearing from God, our flesh or the father of lies? She teaches us how to know which opportunities are from God and which ones to avoid. She teaches how to recognize what "cloaking" is and how to unmask the hidden schemes of the enemy, saving us time, money and frustration.

Jane takes us into the realm of the impossible and shows us what we can do to begin to see the impossible made possible. She does this through narrative and biblical examples and supporting Scripture. Her heart's desire is for the reader to gain a better understanding of the character and nature of God and His desire to interact with us. She reveals to the reader how to access God's promises of provision and how to navigate the details of God's divine directives. Jane points out the importance of time management if we are to have the time to set aside to hear God.

I loved the last three chapters of the book, finding them to be very practical. In these chapters she teaches us how to persevere in hard times and how to stay encouraged in the midst of disappointment. You will learn how God's no may mean something better and how divine declarations position you to receive. You will learn seven ways to reduce the number of errors you make, as well as discovering what you can learn from your mistakes and how to avoid repeating them.

Dr. Jane Glenchur has written a most practical and inspiring book about the possibilities in God and God's possibilities through us. I believe you will be very glad you purchased and read 7 *Secrets to Power Praying: How to Access God's Wisdom and Miracles Every Day.*

Randy Clark, founder and president,
The Apostolic Network
of Global Awakening

Acknowledgments

My highest praises and thanksgiving go to the Lord for creating this book through me, guiding me through every paragraph and opening the doors of opportunity to bring it to publication. To Him be all glory and honor.

To Amelia and Mark—I cherish the wonderful adventures we shared together in following God's breadcrumbs. It was a bumpy road but well worth the trip. I thank my husband, Tom, for his support while I stayed home to raise our children, and for riding over the bumps with us.

Many thanks go to Ryan Atkins for critiquing the content, asking challenging questions, praying and inspiring me.

Without these prayer warriors I could not have seen this book published: Dr. Suelee Jin, Jennifer Odom, Joe and Linda Duffield, Mel Shaffer, Mary Ann Derr, Ron and Cathy Salyer, Diana Stroh, Carol Atkins, Jane Edelmann, Jeannie Handelsmann, Wendy Miller and Patti Younkin. I am also extremely grateful for the prayers of my Oasis family as well as any others that I may have inadvertently failed to mention. God has truly heard your prayers.

My heartfelt gratitude goes to Diane Castelli, Terri Eklund and Ted Mather for teaching me the basics on hearing God; to Joe Ray, my spiritual mentor for many years; to Pastors Tim and Carol Sheets for their spiritual leadership; and to Dr. Charles Heaton, my dermatology professor, who encouraged me to pray for wisdom.

I am very grateful to Dr. Joshua Brown for his expertise; to Ann Weinheimer for her gift in polishing up the text; to Jane Campbell, my editor, for following God's nudges; and to Les Stobbe, my agent, for encouraging a new author.

PART 1

Partnering
with God

1

Miracles in Minutes?

I am not a hobby shopper. Some women salivate at every sale sign and peruse the racks and shelves for entertainment. But for me, shopping is like having my teeth cleaned—a necessity that must be endured. I might still be wearing last decade's styles if God had not infiltrated my aversion to stores, taken the pain out of purchasing—and transformed my understanding of prayer.

It all started with an orange carpet stain. My daughter, who was in elementary school at the time, accidentally spilled juice on the carpet in our family room. Discovering the dried stain days later, I shot up a desperate prayer: "Lord, help me find something to get rid of this stain so that she won't feel bad about the spill (and so I won't be upset!)."

Carpet stain removers lined the lowest shelf of cleaning supplies at Walmart, forcing me to kneel down to examine them. Miraculous claims of stain-cleaning power shouted at me from every can. I pondered all the choices, wondering how to choose the best one. To my relief, hardly a soul graced the store at eight in the morning as I, a usually dignified physician, scooted on my knees sideways down the aisle asking God about stain removers. Did He really care about something so insignificant? Would He be angry if I asked?

With a smidgen of faith and a mountain of self-consciousness, I placed my hand on top of a can of cleaner, closed my eyes and asked God, *Is this the right one?* I waited a few seconds. No answer. What was I expecting, thunder from heaven? I moved on to the next. Nothing. As my hand rested on the fourth can a voice proclaimed, "That is the *best* stain remover." It was an audible voice! An angel? My eyes flew open. I heard it again. "That is the *best* stain remover."

I turned toward the direction of the voice. Two frail-looking, white-haired women were ambling down the aisle toward me—not exactly my concept of angelic beings. I paused, my hand motionless on the can. But as they passed behind me one of the duo declared for the third time, "That is the *best* stain remover." I bought the product and the stain vanished.

That incident revolutionized shopping for me. If God cared about a carpet stain, would it be okay to seek His wisdom for other purchases? I needed to buy shoes for our daughter, for instance. What was the harm in asking? God is omniscient; He would know where to find the perfect fit. After all, nothing rivaled trying to find shoes for Amelia's narrow feet. Her pint-sized patience evaporated in seconds, catalyzing an avalanche of anger in store after store as she tried on dozens of shoes only to leave empty-handed. Since binding her feet was not an option, I despaired at shoe shopping with her.

This, however, was a new day. Before clambering into the car together we asked God to show us where to purchase her new shoes. As we waited expectantly, a certain store came to my mind. Would we really find the right fit on our first try? We decided to test it out. Less than an hour later an adorable pair of new shoes adorned her feet. We were on to something huge.

The next lesson involved Amelia's Christmas present. She had her heart set on a new bicycle to replace the one she had outgrown. Just days before the holiday, I suddenly realized there was only a one-hour window to purchase the bike and hide it before she got home from school. I had no idea what color she wanted or where to buy it. Why had I not checked? Was it expecting too much to ask God for the store *and* the color? Would I be able to hear God in just a few minutes?

I quieted my thoughts and prayed. Pink was her favorite color, but purple was the impression I received. What store had a purple 24-inch girl's bike? In my mind's eye I saw a retailer in an area of town that I normally do not frequent. Desperation and doubt intermixed with faith as I drove to the store and hurried to the sporting goods section. There in the center of the aisle stood a purple 24-inch girl's bike, waiting just for me. *All* the other bikes hung from the wall. God's provision could not have been more obvious. When Amelia received the bicycle on Christmas day, she exclaimed, "Purple is the color I wanted!"

Not only did these experiences help me begin to look at shopping as an adventure and teach me to be a good steward of our finances, but something much greater took place: I sensed that this was just the beginning of learning to pray with power. Would God help with all of our needs, or was there a limit to what we could ask—or how often? If God cared about a bicycle, did He care about healing—or was that too big a request? And how best to pray? Was there some way to access His wisdom and power for answers to our needs every day?

In my apprenticeship of prayer, begun that morning with a stain in the carpet, I learned seven secrets—practical how-to steps to access God's wisdom for personalized answers to prayer.

Some believers have been taught not to bother God unless it is for major decisions like deciding whom to marry or what house to buy or finding the right doctor. Other believers think the opposite—that "big needs" like healing are basically impossible to receive through prayer, so trying for something smaller has a better chance of success.

I cannot find either restriction anywhere in Scripture. The Bible actually says the opposite: "Casting the whole of your care [*all your anxieties, all your worries, all your concerns, once and for all*] on Him, for He cares for you affectionately and cares about you watchfully" (1 Peter 5:7 AMPLIFIED, emphasis added). The Contemporary English Version states it this way: "God cares for you, so turn all your worries over to him." This is a directive, not a suggestion. Besides, what determines how big the problem must be before involving God? Is there a table of weights and measures for prayer in the back of the Bible so that if you are going to purchase something that weighs fewer than a hundred pounds you are on your own, but anything over that is fair game to inquire of the Lord? Or is it futile to pray for migraine headaches, but you can feel confident about praying for a sprained toe? I mean no disrespect, but why limit the Lord when He offers to help us in *all* of our cares and concerns?

Jesus said: "Everyone who asks receives; the one who seeks finds; and to the one who knocks, the door will be opened" (Matthew 7:8). Our part is to ask. Jesus also said: "If you, then, though you are evil, know how to give good gifts to your children, how much more will your Father in heaven give good gifts to those who ask him!" (Matthew 7:11).

His words challenge us to ask God for *anything* that we lack. After all, when our children have needs to be met, my husband, Tom, and I will do whatever we can to meet them. Our heavenly Father says He will do even *much more* for us. I think He means it.

Christ commands us not to worry about what we will eat, drink or wear because He will provide for all of our needs when we seek Him first (see Matthew 6:25–33). Since He promises to supply, why would He not help us find that supply?

Some denominations teach that God stopped speaking to His people; that God no longer communicates through dreams, visions or an inner, quiet voice; that He only speaks to us now through His Word. Where does Scripture say that?

The book of Acts is replete with stories of believers being guided by the Holy Spirit. Jesus Himself said: "It is to your advantage that I go away; for if I do not go away, the Helper will not come to you; but if I depart, I will send Him to you" (John 16:7 NKJV). He also said: "When He, the Spirit of truth, has come, He will guide you into *all truth*; for He will not speak on His own authority, but whatever He hears He will speak; and He will tell you *things to come*" (John 16:13 NKJV, emphasis added). Jesus was talking about the Holy Spirit, whom the believers were instructed to wait for after His resurrection and who filled them to overflowing on the day of Pentecost (see Acts 2:1–4).

It would seem that the Holy Spirit's job description has been markedly restricted if He no longer speaks truth to us and no longer tells us "things to come." It was not just the disciples who received the Spirit of truth, but all 120 believers waiting and praying in the Upper Room, and all of us since then who have placed our faith in Christ as Lord and Savior.

In his book *Surprised by the Voice of God*, Jack Deere describes his journey from unbelieving believer to believing believer. He describes himself as a former cessationist who used to believe the Bible is the *only* way God communicates with man. He focused exclusively on biblical knowledge *apart* from a personal relationship with Christ. Please do not misunderstand. I believe the Bible is the inerrant Word of God. So does Jack Deere. But as he discovered—and I also believe and experience on a regular basis—God still communicates with His people just as He promised He would.

God created us for relationship. He wants His sheep to hear His voice and does not restrict Himself in how He talks to us. Why, then, would we restrict Him? His sheep are ordinary people like you and me. If Jesus says in Scripture that He wants to talk to me, I do not want to miss any of His communications.

The Amplified translation of Jeremiah 33:3 instructs us that when we call upon God, He will not only respond but show us "great and mighty things, fenced in and hidden, which you do not know (do not distinguish and recognize, have knowledge of and understand)."

He demonstrates His love in tangible ways as He supplies our needs. Every detail of our lives matters to Him, and He delights in blessing us. We honor God when we put Him first in everything. I told the story of buying a carpet cleaner, for instance, not to trivialize God, but to illustrate His great love for us. He cares about us because we are His children. Our problems matter to Him. If we are struggling with tough decisions or have needs that we cannot see any way to meet, God will help us make wise choices. *We can access His wisdom and miracles every day.*

I have learned that engaging with God about whatever I am facing stretches my faith. The determination to grow my faith means I must be willing to take risks and give myself grace when I fail. The rewards are well worth it. My mistakes have taught me not to fret, not to move in haste and to wait until I have peace. Asking for God's wisdom has taught me that He is personal, patient and provides much better than I can with my limited human understanding.

That is the heart of this book, learning to partner with God. In so doing, you, too, will develop an intimate relationship with the Lord and experience miraculous answers to prayer.

My challenge to you today is to begin believing that God cares about your concerns—big and small. This is just the beginning of an exciting journey to the heart of God. We will be learning, in the first part of this book, to rethink our limited view of prayer as we partner with Him for answers. In part 2, we will explore seven specific secrets that unleash the power of prayer. Then, in the final part, we will learn tools for putting the seven power secrets into action. I will share many more faith-building stories as we go along to show you how these principles work.

Keep in mind: When you ask for God's help, He receives the glory and your faith multiplies. It is a win-win proposition.

Remember . . .

- No problem or decision is too insignificant for God. Cast all your cares on Him.
- Engaging God throughout the decision-making process grows your faith.
- God's promise to provide for your needs comes with directions, *if you listen.*
- Are you willing to take some risks to partner with God in your everyday decisions?

2

Who Qualifies
for Extraordinary Answers?

When I was in the sixth grade, our family moved from a small town in New Jersey out to the countryside. My father had purchased a home for us built in 1740. The doors fascinated me. Instead of twentieth-century doorknobs, the doors were fitted with wrought-iron latches holding large keys. Since then I have loved keys—and will use that image here to help answer the question of who qualifies for answers to prayer.

Is it a given that only a select few can pray prayers that get answered? No, definitely not. During my prayer apprenticeship, I discovered five keys that anyone can use to unlock the secrets to answered prayer. You can take these keys and start using them right away to help you grow in your relationship with God. Several of them will be discussed in more detail later in the book. The closer you get to God's heart, the more you will be encouraged to seek His wisdom for your needs.

Key #1: Petition

"God, *please* use me. *Please.*" I sat in the bathroom stall pleading with God. There had to be something a freshman medical student could do for Him. With less than a semester of classes behind me, I was heading home to study for exams. Having recommitted my life to Christ the year before while applying to medical school, I was frustrated that nothing extraordinary was happening. The book of Acts was chock full of supernatural events. Why was God not using *me*? I did not want to settle for sitting in church an hour every week. I had done that all my growing-up years. There had to be more to my new life in Christ.

I left the restroom and headed out to the courtyard. One of my new friends, also a Christian, was surrounded by a small group of classmates who were searching the paving stones for something. Apparently Margo had lost a contact lens and did not have a replacement. Exams started the next day, making it imperative to find it.

I joined the group as we knelt and ran our hands over the small area where the lens had fallen. Twenty or thirty minutes passed, and one by one the students gave up until only three of us remained. The setting sun and the pressure to head home to study weighed heavily against my concern for Margo.

I sat down and prayed silently, *Lord, please show me where that contact is. She can't study without it. We really need Your help. We're running out of time.* I sensed and saw nothing. I repeated my plea, but this time when I opened my eyes, the Spirit of the Lord declared, *It's right there.* I was puzzled by the clarity of His words in my spirit in the absence of any evidence of the lens. Nonetheless, I searched intently. Still nothing.

Lord, it's not there, I responded. I prayed again fervently, opened my eyes and heard the same words. I ran my hand slowly over the site. *God, it's not there. I don't understand why You keep saying that it is there.*

Look again. It's there, He replied. Frustrated and wondering if there was something wrong with my spiritual ears, I opened my eyes and looked at the exact same spot. There, glistening like a diamond catching the last of the sun's rays, was the contact lens. It could not have been more obvious or more brilliant, yet seconds before it simply had not been there. I let out a whoop of victory. Margo carefully picked it up. Only upon returning to my car did I realize that God had answered my plea in the restroom.

It would take many more years before I understood the keys to becoming the kind of person who sees more miracles like that one. I did not have to be Mother Teresa or Joan of Arc. But I did have to ask—and keep on asking (see Matthew 7:8 Amplified).

Key #2: Passion

I discovered the second key while attending my first adult Bible study. My pastor's wife had encouraged me to take a course by popular writer and speaker Beth Moore on building the Tabernacle. I was not especially excited about this. *Why would I want to learn about architecture?* I thought, but I signed up on the teacher's promise to show us Jesus in the Old Testament. I had no idea He camped out there. That shows how little I knew about Scripture!

The study included video presentations of Beth Moore's teaching. That first video revealed a key to accessing God's heart. She spoke about the Lord with such passion and intimacy that I clutched at every word like a beggar grasping for a handout. Tears streamed down my cheeks. While others chatted pleasantly with their seatmates, I kept my eyes glued to her face, my ears to her words.

How could she be so excited about Jesus? My denominational church had served Him up like dry toast. Following Christ was an intellectual pursuit; He was someone to be obeyed in order to avoid punishment, not someone to be adored and pursued with passion. Beth Moore's Jesus was totally different from mine, and I was amazed at her promise that we could have a relationship with Him, this One who created the universe. My hunger for a personal connection with Christ translated into a prayer that morning that would change the rest of my life: "Lord, I want the same passion she has."

Up until that prayer, everything about me was logical, linear and analytical. It was the kind of mental processing that served me well in the medical field. Quite frankly, as a keep-to-myself, back-row type of person, passion was not on my emotional palette. I did not know spiritual passion existed until I saw it in Beth Moore. And I had to have it.

"Lord, *make* me passionate about You," became the cry of my heart week after week. I could not generate it, buy it or barter for it. "God, I want the same kind of passion she has." What was I expecting? Was there a switch He would flip if I bugged Him enough? Would I wake up one morning and see Beth's face staring back at me in the mirror?

As the Bible study progressed and she unveiled Jesus in the details of the Tabernacle, my eyes were opened to an amazing, incomprehensible Creator who wove Christ into the fabric of the Old Testament before anyone even knew His name was Jesus. The Word of God had stunning treasures hidden among the pages. Beth mined those spiritual gems and presented them to us. I could not get enough; my appetite was insatiable. The more I heard her teaching, the more excited and passionate I became about the Word and who God is.

God is looking for people who have passion for Him. This key unlocks doors to encounters with God that can be entered no other way. (We will learn how to obtain this passion in chapter 12.)

Key #3: Presence

The person who uses the keys of petition and passion also needs the third key—God's presence. My clinical instructor in medical school used me as an illustration of someone who might easily be misdiagnosed as being hyperthyroid. I raced everywhere. My quickness afoot and my fast-paced attention to patients and even menial "scut work" cleared everyone out of my path. "Slow and steady" was not a concept; "fast and furious" characterized my lifestyle on or off work. I was a medical Martha. Jesus was standing at the door knocking (see Revelation 3:20), but my type-A temperament kept me too preoccupied to slow down and answer—until a malpractice suit knocked me off my feet.

At this point in my life, comfortable in my medical practice, I *thought* my walk with God was pretty solid: church on Sundays, brief prayer at the beginning and end of each day, and prayers at the office for God's wisdom in diagnosing and treating patients and in reading the trays of microscopic slides processed in our laboratory. So how could my name be on that legal piece of paper accusing me of a diagnostic error?

It took a few weeks to let go of the unanswered "Why me?" question and move on to "What do I do now?" My attorney had given me strict limitations about discussing the case with anyone—even within the family—which gave me a lot of time alone with God. Since the Psalms offered the most comfort, I methodically read through them as well as Proverbs, gleaning the verses that spoke loudest to the raging emotions within.

In a short while I had seven typed pages of Scriptures that I read every morning on my knees at 5:30 a.m. This routine accomplished two purposes: I was spending much more time alone in God's presence, and His Word became an absolute necessity to carry me through my day. I clung to His promises of comfort and wisdom the way a novice mountain climber clutches the ropes that secure her to safety. It was a small step toward transitioning from Martha to Mary. The lawsuit taught me to spend more time every day in God's presence.

In the middle of the malpractice suit the Lord impressed upon me to resign my practice. My first thought was, *You must be kidding me.* Surely the stress of preparing for trial was overwhelming enough. Had God forgotten what I had told my husband before we were married—that I would never quit working to stay home and raise a family?

And more than that, did God not understand that I was the main breadwinner at this time, since my husband, an engineer, was working a minimum-wage job while looking for a position? Quitting my practice meant losing most of our income and our insurance. My protests seemed of no consequence to the Lord. I grappled with God for three months, but all my prayers landed me in the same square. Quit now.

Having worked since the age of thirteen, the thought of being a stay-at-home mom, dependent on my husband's employment, frightened me. One of my motivations for pursuing a career in medicine had been financial freedom: I would never have to pinch pennies again. As I mentioned, however, during my application to medical school I had recommitted my life to Christ. Now my career belonged to the Lord. His will had to come first. Even though our children were cared for in our home by my mother, God made it clear that the children needed me home full time. He also had hidden plans for me that could be discovered only by spending more time with Him.

God's way of pursuing more hours with me seemed like a death sentence. And, actually, it was. I died to my career and my independence as a financially secure physician.

Then things began to change. By God's grace, the lawsuit was dropped ten months after it was initiated. Over the next few years as I refashioned my Martha lifestyle to include more and more Mary moments, I had time for the Beth Moore Bible study, a class on how to hear God and an intercessory prayer group. My Mary times excited me far more than the Martha ones had. A whole new world opened, and God was at the center of it. Prayer groups and listening to God became the highlights of my week.

God is looking for people who want to spend time in His presence. Where had this key been hidden all these years? No one had told me that God actually wants to talk to us when we pray. Amazing! Learning to spend time in God's presence—waiting, watching and listening for any form of communication from Him—energized me. Yes, I sometimes felt frustrated if nothing seemed to be happening, but it never grew old.

Spending time in His presence is one of the most important keys to accessing wise counsel. It is life changing. For me, it became as vital as the air I breathe. We will look at this in more detail in later chapters.

Key #4: Preparedness

There is a scene in the movie *Facing the Giants* in which a man who has been praying for local high school students for years confronts the distraught coach of a losing football team with a hypothetical scenario: If two farmers were praying for rain, to whom do you think the Lord would send the rain? To the one who prepared his fields for planting, or the one who did not?

God's heart longs to pour out blessings like rain on His children, but how do we prepare our fields? More than a decade ago I sensed that someday I would be writing for publication, but the timing never seemed right. When our teenage son, Mark, was awarded a scholarship to an out-of-state Christian writing conference, my thoughts about writing resurfaced, and I asked the Lord if this was His timing for me to begin. Having peace that indeed I should go along, not only as a chaperone but also as a participant in the workshops, I signed up and made our plane reservations. It was time to prepare my field.

I spent all day in classes on writing techniques, editing and the many aspects of getting published. After four days of cramming my head full of facts, it was clear that my field needed more plowing and weeding before God's rain could produce a publishable piece. So year after year I returned to the conference to take additional classes on honing my writing skills until it was time to start planting. Preparing our fields may take days, weeks or even years, but the work is necessary for His plans and purposes to take root in our lives.

Ryan, a 24-year-old university student, has been confined to a wheelchair for the last three years, the result of an auto accident that left him paralyzed from the shoulders down. Months after the accident his doctors declared emphatically that he would never walk again. Ryan and his mother, however, received numerous confirmations of God's plan to heal him completely. To prepare his field, Ryan goes through twice daily stretching exercises and physical therapy several times a week. He is maintaining the strength and flexibility of his muscles in preparation for walking and using his arms. His diligent preparation is paying off. He is now beginning to regain movement in his extremities.

It is important to distinguish preparedness from presumption. God initiated the plans for me to write and for Ryan to walk. We are each taking the steps, in His timing, to be prepared for what God has called us to. Presumption occurs when we generate an idea on our own and then set about to accomplish it in our flesh. We are in danger of presumption when we rely on our reasoning without the guidance of the Holy Spirit—when we move ahead in *our* timing using *our* methods of producing results, not His. Zeal for the Lord must be submitted to Him to guard against our presuming that our plans are His plans. Many in the Body of Christ are running around creating programs and activities that never originated in the heart of God.

Incredible joy and peace accompany the Lord's plans for us. In contrast, busyness and stress go hand in hand with presumptive plans that we manufacture to please God or earn others' approval. We might miss God's will if we are busy in the wrong places. That is why it is so important to prepare the field the Lord has given you.

Key #5: Perseverance

I love the acronym PUSH: *Pray until something happens.* Jill Briscoe spoke at a conference I attended many years ago. I will always remember her warning: "You Americans give up too easily," she said. "Pray until something happens!" There are many times when I want to give up. That is when I ask for God's grace to help me persevere to the end. We cannot pray relentlessly in our own strength.

Read what the Amplified version of Philippians 4:13 says: "I have strength for all things in Christ Who empowers me [I am ready for anything and equal to anything through Him Who infuses inner strength into me; I am self-sufficient in Christ's sufficiency]." All the strength and energy we need are in Christ who lives in us and who releases it when we ask.

Amelia had frequent ear infections as a young child, necessitating three sets of tubes in her ears. The last set left a hole in one eardrum. Although the ear specialist suggested closing it surgically, we prayed that God would heal it. Years after the infections stopped she noticed a funny noise in that ear. When we asked God what it was, I heard Him say, *I am healing her ear.*

At her next pediatrician's appointment we expected the doctor to declare it was healed, but to our surprise she noted that the perforation had not changed.

What was going on? I was certain I had heard God correctly. I persisted in praying and declaring healing over that ear, despite the pediatrician's repeat diagnosis at every annual exam.

Four years after hearing God's promise, we returned to the ear specialist for a different concern. He peered into Amelia's ear canal and announced: "The perforation is healed." It is wonderful when God's promises manifest immediately, but many times they require perseverance in prayer.

Who Qualifies? You Do!

Petition, passion, presence, preparedness and perseverance are the main keys anyone—not just a special few—can use to open the door of God's favor and see extraordinary answers to prayer. These keys enable you and me to partner with God to fulfill our destinies. They unlock the secret treasures of His wisdom so that we can make godly choices every day for ourselves and our families.

The day I closed the door to my medical practice, I had no idea what God had in store for me. Sixteen years later I realize that no amount of money could buy the spiritual wisdom and discernment that God has provided me with. I relinquished riches and found what is priceless.

What about you? Do you doubt that your prayers can be answered? Would you like that to change? How much of God do you want? Be honest. If you are ambivalent, *petition* Him to make you single-mindedly focused on Him. God is captivated when we pursue Him with *passion*. He will ignite a yearning for His *presence*, if you ask. *Persevere* until it manifests. Begin to *prepare* your heart and mind by reading His Word. Extraordinary answers to your prayers are waiting to be released from heaven.

Remember . . .

- Passionate petitions garner God's attention.
- Spending time in God's presence is vital to receiving wise counsel.
- Preparing your fields positions you for godly windows of opportunity.
- Will you persevere and pray until God releases His answer?

3

Google or God?

Google or God—where do we go first for answers? In this age of technology, the Internet has become the default source of wisdom for making decisions. Have we replaced God with a computer when we really need to learn how to access the Author of all knowledge? Youth especially have grown up clutching a mouse instead of a parent's hand in prayer. Technology seems to have taken priority over a better source of wisdom. Whom do you search first, Google or God?

I typed *fear of flying help* into the search window today. Google produced 18,400,000 results. Eight years ago I prayed one prayer and God healed me of my fear of flying in fewer than fifteen minutes. Here is what happened.

After terrorists hijacked American jetliners and struck the World Trade Center, I refused to board a plane for the next four years. While I was praying with a friend one day the Lord told me He wanted to heal my fear. My response? "I don't want to be healed. If He heals me, I will have to fly, and I don't want to fly."

My logic was no match for His divine wisdom. With my friend's encouragement, I agreed to cooperate with God. The Lord showed me that the design of a jet plane originated with Him. Then He challenged me with this question: *Would you like to see Me take one apart and put it together again? I know where every part goes.* He began to impress on my mind the intricacy of a jet plane until I trusted the fact that if He could invent something so complicated, He could ensure my safety while flying in it. I gave Him my fear and asked Him to remove it. He did. God had an ulterior motive in healing me. Right afterward, He directed me to fly to an out-of-state medical conference where divine appointments awaited me.

We can research our options and find the most logical approach to a problem, but we need to be mindful that not every logical idea originates in the heart of God. This has been a major part of my prayer apprenticeship. As I read Scripture and ask God to direct my thoughts, He transforms my mind. When I need to make a decision I submit the issue to the Lord and ask for His guidance. The next step is crucial—listening for His directions. This is where many believers miss God's will and His best for their lives. They assume that after they ask for wisdom they do not need to listen.

When Christians meet to solve a problem, for instance, we often begin with a prayer for wisdom—but then the rest of the session consists of batting ideas around the table. Brainstorming is not a sin, but what is missing? If we reach a decision, do we stop to confirm that our final choice is His will for us? A consensus of believers does not guarantee that our solution is His answer to the problem.

Better yet, why not "Google" God first and simply ask, "Lord, what would You have us do in this situation?" When we quiet our minds and listen for His heart, God often saves us time by providing novel solutions up front that are extraordinarily better than what we can dream up. If He is silent, we can proceed with brainstorming, but still leave the final choice to Him. Might meetings be faster, more efficient and led by the Holy Spirit?

During my early apprenticeship years in power praying, I sought God, received His directions and then dragged my feet, all because His logic was illogical to me. I found myself responding with "God, that doesn't make sense" far too many times. Yet every time I obeyed it made perfect sense in retrospect. Romans 8:6–7 explains why:

> Now the mind of the *flesh* [which is *sense and reason without the Holy Spirit*] is death [death that comprises all the miseries arising from sin, both here and hereafter]. But the mind of the [Holy] Spirit is life and [soul] peace [both now and forever]. [That is] because the *mind of the flesh* [with its carnal thoughts and purposes] *is hostile to God*, for it does not submit itself to God's Law; indeed it cannot.
>
> Amplified, emphasis added

Without the Holy Spirit guiding our thinking, our minds will produce thoughts that are in opposition to God. Believers can be filled with the Holy Spirit and still have fleshly thoughts, but as we mature spiritually our minds are progressively renewed by the Word of God. As that Word takes root in our hearts, it changes our way of thinking and making decisions so that carnal thoughts are fewer and fewer. We are not to conform to the world, but to be transformed into the image of Christ by the renewing of our minds with Scripture so that we will know His perfect will for us (see Romans 12:2).

Notice again that Romans 8:6 states that the mind of the flesh is "sense and reason *without* the Holy Spirit" (emphasis added). Jesus modeled the way God wants us to live our lives. He spent long hours in the night seeking His Father's will through prayer and listening. He did only what God directed Him to do (see John 5:30). He did not sit with the disciples and brainstorm; He sought God.

Jesus had to leave earth in order for the Holy Spirit to come dwell in us (see John 16:7). Why is the Holy Spirit so vital to believers? In addition to being a comforter, God's Spirit guides us into *all* truth and tells us things that will happen in the *future* (see John 16:13). Through Him we have direct access to the unlimited wisdom of our Creator, to the one true God who sees all, knows all and is never too busy to guide and direct us in every situation. What more do we need to make wise decisions, to be in the center of God's will for ourselves and our families? Google might provide millions of "answers," but God will provide the one *right* answer. Why settle for the limitations of our human minds when we can access perfect answers to our problems?

What Role Does Logic Play?

Mankind's first mistake was relying solely on logic and reasoning. God gave Adam and Eve permission to eat the fruit of any tree in the Garden of Eden, except the Tree of Knowledge of Good and Evil. But when the serpent (Satan) questioned Eve in order to deceive her, he asked, "Did God really say, 'You must not eat from any tree in the garden'?" (Genesis 3:1).

How did Eve respond? First, she reiterated what God had told Adam not to do. What happened next is very important. Eve looked at the forbidden tree, saw that it was good for food, that it was attractive and that it would make her wise (see Genesis 3:6). Eve had not forgotten God's directions. No, Eve used logic and reasoning to determine that eating the fruit would be a better choice than obeying God.

Logic is not always our best option—in fact, God's directions might seem to defy human logic. Have you ever, for instance, tried to apply logic to some of the stories in the Old Testament? At God's direction Abraham packed up his family and possessions to move, having no idea where God would lead them (see Hebrews 11:8). How many of us would be willing to explain that to our relatives? What about Elisha throwing a stick into a river to make an iron axhead rise to the surface after it had fallen into the water (see 2 Kings 6:6)? Elisha threw flour into a pot of poisoned food and neutralized the poison so that no one died (see 2 Kings 4:41). Do any of these make sense?

Let's look at the New Testament. The wine ran out at a wedding. Jesus told the servants to fill large pots with water and take them to the manager of the banquet. Without His even touching the water it turned to wine (see John 2:7–9). Jesus instructed Peter to take the first fish he caught, open its mouth and take the coin he found there to pay their taxes (see Matthew 17:27). What about Paul's handkerchief? Just by touching it, people were healed and delivered (see Acts 19:12). And in four years of medical school we never learned about healing blindness by using mud or spit (see John 9:6–7). None of Jesus' miracles is logical.

The Bible is filled with true accounts of ordinary people being led by God to do illogical acts that produced supernatural results. Are we missing out on miracles because we limit ourselves to human logic and reasoning?

On one mission trip to Brazil, I was asked to pray for an eight-year-old boy who had been unable to breathe through his nostrils since birth. This was a time when my faith was barely perceptible. My medical mind reasoned briefly that it would be impossible to unblock both nares, but I chose to pray anyway.

First, I verified that no air was moving through either nostril. Then I prayed and checked again. Some air moved over my finger. As I persisted in praying, the blockage diminished progressively until it disappeared completely. We were surprised and overjoyed. Had I leaned on my logic and professional training, I would have referred him to an ear, nose and throat specialist, and missed a miracle.

We have all heard the expression, "God gave you a brain; use it." But how does God want us to use it? Romans 8:9 tells us that we are living godly lives when the Holy Spirit "dwells within you [*directs and controls you*]" (AMPLIFIED, emphasis added). Are we setting aside enough time to know the Word of God and to be directed and controlled by His Spirit? Investing time in learning to hear God positions us to be in the right place at the right time. We are well advised to follow Christ's example: Jesus immersed Himself in prayer long before the sun came up in order to prepare for His day (see Mark 1:35). How much more ought we to do the same! God is teaching me that consecrating my mind daily to His purposes, submitting my decisions to Him and *listening* to His guidance make a world of difference in making wise choices and seeing miracles.

Jesus did only what He saw His heavenly Father do (see John 5:19). We are instructed to do the same (see Ephesians

5:1). Only God knows the future. The Holy Spirit will lead us step by step with unlimited wisdom and efficiency, far beyond the boundaries of our human reasoning.

I saw this principle at work when our son had apprehension about an overnight camping trip when he was in the fourth grade. God had a special surprise in store when Mark arrived at the lodge. He told me later what happened. "Mom, it was incredible," he said. "I had already seen every detail of the building—the clock over the fireplace, the layout of the rooms—everything! It was all exactly the way God showed me." God's Spirit had prepared him in advance in order to alleviate his fears. In the natural, experiences like this do not make sense, but they increase our faith in a supernatural, personal, loving God.

Do I throw common sense out the window? No. But by developing a listening ear, I have become sensitive to checks or tugs in my spirit throughout the day. When I hesitate about a decision, I pray, "Lord, is this Your best solution?" He either confirms the common-sense approach or substitutes a better answer. The Holy Spirit has trumped my human reasoning and logic and provided better solutions hundreds of times. We must learn to pace ourselves and keep one ear open to the Lord's directions, or find a quiet place to lay our problems before the Lord and then listen to His directives.

Right Brain versus Left

Two essential tools enable us to access divine wisdom. First, we must learn to flip the switch from our "left brain" to our "right brain" to maximize receptivity to the Holy Spirit. There is no switch, of course, but we can learn to activate the right hemisphere of our brains to hear from God.

Here is what I mean. Logical, linear thinkers are predominantly activating their left hemispheres when solving problems. They want everything to make sense. If this sounds like you, there is hope. My first attempts to hear God frustrated me. As soon as I explained my problem to God and tried to listen, my human reasoning chattered away, offering logical answers and an analysis of which ones made the most sense. My left brain drowned out God's voice, blocking me from hearing His unique solution. God could not get a word in edgewise for all the self-talk my brain was doing.

I still struggle with this at times. Recently I prayed about whether or not to attend a certain conference and heard myself following this line of thought: *I've attended the same meeting the last five years in a row. There's no reason to go this year. I don't know anyone else who is going. It's a nine-hour drive. The hotels are probably booked up by now. I'd get a lot more done if I stayed at home, and I'd save a lot of money.* My dependence on human reasoning and rational decision-making was leading me to conclude that going to the conference would be the wrong choice.

When I became aware, however, that my brain was screening my choices and directing me to a conclusion, I quieted my thoughts. By turning off the logic filter, my mind became peaceful. In the ensuing silence I focused on God and listened for Him to speak. I was willing to allow novel ideas to float into my mind without prescreening. This is what I heard: *You will have an awesome time at the conference. Get excited.* Then I had an impression that God had divine appointments lined up for me. God's perspective transformed my apathy to enthusiasm.

The conference turned out to be amazing. I met the editorial director and marketing manager of the publishing company for this book; I had no idea they would be at the conference when I registered for it. My path also intersected those of other key people with whom I will have future connections related to my career in writing and dermatology. It paid to listen to His plans and not my own.

Our brains have billions of nerve cells (neurons) that make trillions of connections with each other. When we learn something new our brains create pathways between the appropriate neurons. The more we practice a new skill, for instance, the stronger the pathway becomes and the faster and easier it is to do. By trial and error I learned to quiet my logical, reasoning thoughts and listen to God. In other words, I stopped my thoughts from processing and analyzing known data and learned to relax and focus on the Lord. I learned to access a "listening" state of the brain.

Participants in non-Christian forms of meditation learn to access this brainset as well; however, they are not learning to listen to the Holy Spirit. As Christians, we are cautioned not to empty our minds, as the enemy of our souls will gladly fill that vacuum with his lies and deceptions (see Matthew 12:43–45). Rather we are instructed to renew our minds with God's truth (see Romans 12:2). In order to access God's truth and wisdom, we need for our spirits to connect intentionally with His Holy Spirit.

I discovered during a watercolor class that doing something artistic or creative silences the left-brain chatter and activates my right brain, turning off the logic filter and producing amazing peacefulness. Looking at nature, going for a walk or focusing on a mental image of the Lord will "flip that switch" for me as well.

If you sit down to pray and listen to God and find yourself talking inside your head, you are not in the receptive mindset needed to hear Him. Be patient. You can learn to quiet your self-talk. If a to-do list starts running through your thoughts, write it down. Ask God to quiet your flesh. As you practice listening, this will become easier. Focus on listening in your heart, not your head. Over time you will learn to recognize His still, small voice. If you are concerned about hearing the wrong voice, we will talk about how to obtain confirmations in chapter 12.

In the next chapter we are going to learn the second tool for accessing God's wisdom—learning the many ways that God communicates with us as we quiet our hearts and minds. It is almost impossible to access divine wisdom if we are unable to hear Him speak.

Remember . . .

- God's solutions to your problems will often defy human logic.
- You can learn to ask for God's wisdom and hear His response.
- The Holy Spirit will guide you to the truth if you invite Him into your decision making.
- Why settle for the limitations of your human mind when God has perfect answers?

4

Is God on Your Contact List?

"Does God really speak to people?" The question from a woman in my Bible study had more than an edge of disbelief. Her tone, like a glove slapped against my cheek, seemed like a challenge to a spiritual duel. My pulse accelerated. No one had asked me that question point blank before. Those of us who heard God tended to keep that secret close to our chests for fear of ostracism in the mainline denominational churches (where this study was being held). Lying was out, but I did not relish the thought of discussing this issue in a room of possible doubters. If I said yes, would the class think I was crazy? I stalled for time.

"We'll get to that later," I replied. The fear of man won out momentarily over the fear of the Lord.

Does God really speak to us today? If a tree falls in a forest and no one is there to hear it, does it make a sound? Yes. Just so, God is speaking, but many times we miss it because we are not attuned to His voice. Perhaps you are saying, "But God never speaks to *me*." Are you expecting Him to talk, or are you not sure how to listen with spiritual ears yet?

When my cell phone rings, it is my habit to ignore phone numbers that are not on my contact list. Are you ignoring God (or missing a divine appointment) because you do not recognize His call? Is God even on your contact list?

Does God have access to your spiritual inbox day or night? If you woke up at three a.m. would you even consider that it might be God trying to get your attention? If you had a dream, would you think that God was trying to tell you something? If you were driving and a thought ran through your mind to call someone, would you consider that God might be talking to you? Could He be speaking to you through a stranger or even a child?

One afternoon as our family left our favorite restaurant, our then-four-year-old son asked, "Mom, when are you going to buy new tires?"

What an odd question! I thought. *Why would he ask me that?* We had not talked about cars, much less tires, during dinner.

The next day my husband and I stopped to fill up the gas tank in my car. I hate checking the tire pressure, so I asked Tom if he would mind doing it for me. We pulled over to the air pump. A few minutes later his head popped up in my window.

"Do you realize your tires are bald?"

Immediately we remembered our son's question the day before. God was warning me about the dangerous condition of my tires, but I had dismissed it as a silly question from a tiny tot.

The other evening while driving home from a prayer meeting, I began thinking about a friend. We had not spoken in weeks. My brief prayer asking God to give her guidance did not pacify my thoughts, as if unfinished business remained in the spiritual realm. *Does God want me to call her?* I thought. At the next red light I opened my phone to dial her number and noticed that she had called me twenty minutes before. I pulled over onto a side road to pray with her. Her heart was heavy with family issues, and God gave comfort and guidance as we prayed together. I drove home marveling at how God brought her to mind at just the right time.

Many years ago I attended a Messianic Jewish service. A stranger sitting next to me leaned over and said, "Myrrh has to be crushed to release its fragrance." That might seem odd to you, but it spoke volumes to my emotions and brought comfort in the midst of a difficult personal situation I was facing at that time. God used a stranger to acknowledge that yes, my life was in a crushing experience for the moment, but something spiritually sweet would emerge if I did not resist His discipline.

How Does God Communicate Today?

If God used a donkey to speak to Balaam and a burning bush to talk to Moses, is there any limit to His creativity in communicating His wisdom to His people? Some of the more common modes are Scripture, an inner voice, images, impressions, dreams and songs. He may also speak through believers, nonbelievers and through circumstances.

Most believers are not taught how to listen, or even that God still speaks to His children. If we know that God wants to converse with us, and if we take time each day to listen, we will be amazed how often He does communicate.

Why would God speak to Peter in a trance-like vision, direct Joseph with dreams and address Samuel with an audible voice if He did not want us to know some of His ways of communicating with us? The God of the Old and New Testaments is the same God who speaks to us today. He says: "I the LORD do not change" (Malachi 3:6).

Scripture

One of the most common ways that God speaks to His people is through His Word. "All Scripture is God-breathed and is useful for teaching, rebuking, correcting and training in righteousness" (2 Timothy 3:16). Early in my apprenticeship I needed motivation to dust off my Bible and read it. The solution? Day after day I asked God to give me love for His Word until I began to look forward to mining the gems waiting there. Scripture has the power to transform our lives (see Hebrews 4:12), but only if we open the book and study it.

How does God speak to us personally through Scripture? He might bring a particular verse to mind when we need His direction. I grew up in northern New Jersey, so driving snow-covered roads does not bother me. One night before a prayer service, snow fell in sheets and the roads iced over. Unsure whether to step out in faith and trust God to keep me safe or to stay home, I prayed for wisdom. Proverbs 27:12 came to mind: "The prudent see danger and take refuge, but the simple keep going and pay the penalty." God was warning me not to chance the drive. To have ignored that Scripture would have been presumption. On another snowy day, however, when schools were canceled, God directed me to drive to a friend's house to pray. Though I was leery at first, He confirmed my safekeeping in multiple ways. The key to my safety was dependence upon Him and following His directives.

A few nights ago I awoke in the wee hours of the morning with the number 3247 in the forefront of my mind. I could have passed it off as a quirky thought and fallen back asleep. Not wanting to miss anything God has to say, though, I grabbed my Bible and discovered there are only two books in the Bible that have a chapter 32 and verse 47. Deuteronomy 32:47 refers to the time the Israelites were about to cross into the Promised Land. God used that verse to reassure me that promises He made to me years ago are about to be fulfilled.

Once I awoke at 8:28 a.m. Immediately the Lord impressed upon me to read Romans 8:28. That verse brought me needed comfort at that time. Please do not misunderstand, I am not looking for spiritual meaning every time I look at a clock, but I do pay attention when I sense the Holy Spirit is speaking to me.

Here is another example of how God's Word speaks to us. Pregnancy eluded me despite years of infertility treatments. Pangs of sadness and frustration surged through me at the sight of a pregnant woman. One day I randomly turned to Genesis 30. The first and only Scripture that I read there was verse 22: "Then God remembered Rachel; he listened to her and enabled her to conceive." Those words instantly took root in my heart. I had never before sensed power and personal significance connected to a verse. From that moment on, whenever I saw a pregnant woman, I quietly declared, "*All things are possible with God. All things.*" I had a 5 percent chance of getting pregnant. That statistic meant nothing to God. Four years later I gave birth to a son.

Genesis 30:22 was a *rhema* ("utterance," Greek) word to me—it was meant to be received by faith before it manifested and to be warred over with persistent prayer. A rhema word is a Scripture that the Holy Spirit highlights and plants in our hearts. It is a promise that pops off the page and waits to be fulfilled when we stand in faith, declaring its truth despite its supposed impossibility. God's Word is the food that feeds our spirits and produces faith that His promises to us will come to pass.

Please note that rhema words are conditional on our faith and obedience. Ten of the twelve spies that scouted out the Promised Land died in the wilderness, and the Israelites wandered for forty years in the desert because they did not add their faith to God's promise. So, too, we must add our faith to the promises that God gives us.

The admonition *No Bible, no breakfast* is the best motivator for me to read the Word every morning before I start my day and before I pick up my cell phone. Distractions and busyness too easily steal my time unless I adhere to that discipline. If you do not have a solid knowledge of Scripture, now is a great time to start reading and studying the Word. I encourage you to join a Bible study in order to mine on a regular basis the riches hidden within those pages.

An Inner Voice

God often speaks to me through an inner voice. If I were to tell you to say the word *giraffe* in your mind, it would be similar to how the inner voice of God sounds—like your own voice except the content is from the Lord. I may hear that inner voice when I am actively listening in prayer for specific guidance, or it might pop into my head at unexpected moments.

Many times during my medical training, as I exited the hospital and headed toward my car, a "little voice" would tell me to go back and see a certain patient. Back then I had no idea it was God directing me. When I obeyed and returned, I discovered that the patient needed attention right then. Unfortunately, there were times my exhaustion talked me out of obeying that inner voice.

When an un-churched friend needed wisdom I suggested that we pray. It was the first time he heard God give him specific information. Minutes later as we prepared to part ways he commented, "I think God is talking to us all the time. We just aren't listening." He heard God easily because he had not been biased by church doctrine telling him that God no longer speaks.

Focus on what the Lord told the Israelites when they came out of Egypt: "But this thing I did command them: *Listen to and obey My voice*, and I will be your God and you will be My people; and walk in the whole way that I command you, that it may be well with you" (Jeremiah 7:23 AMPLIFIED, emphasis added).

God did not ask; He commanded His people to listen to His voice. In the Old Testament God communicated mainly through a select group—the prophets and the priests. With the outpouring of the Holy Spirit at Pentecost, however, all believers are enabled to hear His voice.

Jesus said, "My sheep listen to my voice; I know them, and they follow me" (John 10:27). Christ dwells in each believer (His sheep) through His Holy Spirit. Why would He say that we hear His voice, if He is not speaking to us? When God says "Listen to and obey My voice," we must position ourselves to hear by listening intentionally when we pray. Most times we miss His voice because we simply are not expecting God to speak.

When my daughter says she will be home at five p.m. for supper, I start looking at the clock around that time and listening for the sound of her car pulling into the garage. I am expecting her to show up, so my ears are attuned to the sounds of her arrival. In the same way, when I pray, I anticipate hearing God give me guidance, so my spiritual antennae are ready to perceive His voice. If we believe that God speaks only through the Bible, we will not be looking or listening for any other form of communication.

One day as I sat observing my children on the playground I heard the words *ministry to children* spoken into my spirit. *Ministry to children?* I thought. *That's not for me.* I had no particular connection with children other than my own. Suddenly a young boy ran over to me in tears and threw himself into my arms. Although dazed by this unexpected event, I comforted him until his tears vanished and he happily rejoined his friends. *What was that all about?* I wondered.

Years later I served on the adult leadership team for a youth mission trip. One of the Brazilian interpreters looked at me and declared, "Ministry to children." God confirmed through a stranger what I had heard years earlier through an inner voice. On that trip God instilled within me a love for teens and young adults. One of my passions now is mentoring young people.

Images

Many times God creates an image in my mind's eye to communicate His message. I was driving home one day, for example, when the brake light lit up on the dashboard. Should

I continue driving or pull over? Would the brake pads mal-function at the next stop? When I asked the Lord what was happening, I saw a picture of a partially emptied brake fluid canister and a small cut in the line. From that impression, He assured me that it was safe to continue driving. When I took the car in for repairs, I was told that the brake fluid level was low due to a slow leak in the system.

On another occasion while praying about an upcoming flight to Washington, D.C., I saw myself talking to a young woman with dark, curly shoulder-length hair. My natural inclination when traveling is to settle in with a good book rather than chat with strangers. Why would God want me to connect with this particular woman?

On the afternoon of the flight I saw no one matching that description in the waiting area, so I boarded the plane with—I admit—relief. With the seat next to mine empty, I was ready to settle in for a quiet, restful flight. Then, just before the door closed, in rushed a young woman with dark, shoulder-length curly hair, exactly like the woman God had shown me. Guess where her seat was located? Right next to mine. By the time the plane landed she had shared why she had left the church and the spiritual struggles she was dealing with. This conversation never would have happened if the Lord had not prepared me. I would have dozed off or read a few chapters. The image God gave me in advance made all the difference in my actions.

Most of the pictures I receive from God occur when I pray with my eyes closed. These are called closed visions. In a closed vision, I can look around and explore the image in my mind's eye. Often other details will become apparent by asking God to show me more. Occasionally I will see an image that appears to exist in the natural realm (with my eyes open), but it disappears in seconds. This is an open vision.

Like dreams, the pictures God gives may be literal or symbolic. They often require prayer to interpret what He is communicating. One time, for example, God directed a friend to step down from a leadership position at church to write a book. She wondered if signing up for a Bible study would take up too much of her time. When we prayed, God gave me a picture of an electrical outlet with the number 1 next to it, meaning the study would be her one weekly outlet with people.

If a picture does not make sense, be careful not to dismiss it without first asking God for confirmation and interpretation.

Impressions

An impression is a concept that occurs spontaneously and is not the result of deliberate thought. It is often unrelated to what one is doing or thinking at the time.

My daughter hears God primarily through impressions. One day while driving to her internship she had an impression to stop at a fast-food restaurant. This made no sense since she had brewed too much coffee that morning and had no desire for another cup. But the thought persisted and she obeyed. She placed an order for a breakfast sandwich, and as she inched forward in the drive-through lane, she noticed that the driver of the car behind her was a military man. She felt a distinct urge to pay for his order. Being on a tight budget she hesitated for a moment, but the notion persisted and she decided to obey.

When she reached the cashier's window, she said, "I would like to pay the bill for the gentleman behind me. How much is his order?"

"Seven dollars and seventy-seven cents," the young lady replied.

Amelia had just enough money to cover both orders and handed it all over. The number seven in the Bible symbolizes divine perfection. Amelia took that as confirmation that she had heard correctly and paid his bill, but not before writing a note on his receipt, *Thanks for your service.* The surprised look on his face made the sacrifice worth every penny.

On another occasion Amelia was running errands when she felt an impression to go to a particular fast-food restaurant. She was not hungry or thirsty. It made no sense. But the thought kept recurring, so she obeyed. She ordered a soft drink, sat down and wondered, *Why am I here, Lord?*

Shortly thereafter, a woman with three children in tow noticed my daughter's sweatshirt, emblazoned with the name of the Christian university she attended. She introduced herself and asked if Amelia wanted a part-time nanny job. Did she ever! This connection led to yet another babysitting job, all because she obeyed an impression that did not make sense in the natural.

How do we discern if an impression originates from God or our own minds? Sometimes only time will tell. In 1990, my husband and I flew to Romania to adopt two children. While we were trying to adopt a two-year-old girl named Anca, Tom would occasionally comment, "I think we're here to get the paper work ready for someone else to adopt her." This made no sense to us. Why fly all the way to Eastern Europe to enable someone else to adopt her? He could not explain it. It was just an impression. After locating Anca's mother and securing her signature on the necessary documents, we found out that her father lived in Florida. We needed his signature, too. Had we reached a dead end?

We returned home with the father's name and address and sought help from our Romanian neighbor, George. "No problem. I will call the father for you." We listened as George presented our case to Anca's father in Romanian. He hung up the phone with a smile and told us that Anca's father agreed to sign the papers. Weeks later, however, we still had nothing from him. We sought George's help again.

"No problem," he replied. "I have a cousin in the same town in Florida as the father. I will ask him to take the papers to him."

"But, George, the documents have to be notarized," I explained.

"No problem, my cousin is a notary."

We had our signed, notarized release shortly thereafter. At that point, however, we discovered that Anca had a serious kidney problem that might require a transplant. Our insurance would not cover any preexisting conditions. After wrestling in prayer for weeks we finally released her to the Lord, having no peace to continue the adoption. It looked as though our trip had been a failure. I prayed that God would place her in a Christian family.

Months later we learned that a couple from Israel had adopted her immediately, a process that normally took a month or more in Romania. My husband's impression was correct after all: God used us to do what that Israeli couple could not have done. We readied Anca's file for someone else to adopt her. God also answered my prayer—her adoptive parents are Christians—and God graciously gave us another little girl.

If you receive an impression that seems to come from outside yourself and does not violate Scripture, ask God to confirm if it is from Him, or remove it if it is not from Him.

Dreams

Dreams are treasures wrapped up in night parables. When our bodies are asleep, all the distractions and filters that block out God during the waking hours are suppressed, giving the Lord free access to our minds. God uses dreams to show us emotions that we need to deal with, solutions to problems, witty inventions, warnings and future events, to name a few things.

It is not my intent to go into detail about how to interpret dreams, as there are numerous books on dream interpretation (see appendix C: Suggested Reading). I have, however, found that if a dream is still fresh in my mind when I awake, it is from God. The others disappear instantly. I keep a journal of my dreams and their interpretations, as God frequently speaks to me during the night.

I have received many job offers in my sixteen years of being a stay-at-home mom. One lucrative offer came when my husband was unemployed and money was in short supply. It was particularly tempting. I inquired of the Lord whether or not to accept it. That night I had a dream in which God showed me some undesirable behind-the-scenes details of that job, confirming what I suspected but wanted to ignore for the sake of easing the strain on our budget. I declined the offer.

Right before I left on a youth mission trip, my daughter had a dream in which she warned me not to follow the "night light." I prayed but did not receive an interpretation before leaving.

On the trip, one young man came to me and asked if we could discuss a situation involving several other team members. We sat down at a nearby table, where he happened to take a seat under a bright light while my chair was in shadows.

As he explained the problem I heard the Lord warn me repeatedly, *Night light, night light.* This was my cue to bow out of the situation and hand it to someone higher in authority. As the story unraveled, I saw God's hand of protection and was grateful for the warning in the dream.

If you are one who says, "I never dream," ask God to start speaking to you in dreams. Many times my children have complained, "Mom, I'm not hearing God anymore." Yet they are having dreams in which He is communicating with them. Keep a journal on your nightstand to record your dreams immediately upon awakening. If you fall back asleep without writing them down, you might forget them when you awaken later.

Songs

At times God advises me through songs or hymns. Suppose, for example, I ask the Lord if something important needs to be done today or if it can wait another day. I might hear the refrain from the song "Tomorrow." Then I have peace about scheduling it for the next day. If I am not sure that God wants me to speak with someone about an issue, the words from the hymn "Let All Mortal Men Keep Silent" might play in my head, and I know that God is telling me not to mention it. If you hear a song when you pray for wisdom, note how the words or title of the song might relate to your situation.

Circumstances

A word of caution is necessary here. I find that circumstances are the least reliable means of hearing God, although He does use them. Satan easily manipulates circumstances. Be cautious about relying on them for making decisions. Putting too much emphasis on trying to interpret circumstances and relate them to our life situations can border on superstition. I try not to make any important decisions based solely on circumstantial events, but seek God for additional confirmation.

One day I was quite a distance from my local grocery store when I decided to stop at a supermarket to pick up an item before heading home. As I made a beeline for the product, I noticed a mom I know who has an adopted daughter. We had not spoken in years. I knew instantly that this was not a coincidence. I changed directions and engaged her in conversation. Sure enough she was struggling with some adoption issues. It was a God-given opportunity to share wisdom He had given me in raising our adopted daughter. She expressed her gratitude and relief as we parted. Running into people unexpectedly tends to be the most common way that I see God speaking to me in my circumstances.

In another instance as I was crying out to the Lord over an issue and getting nowhere spiritually, I turned left at a four-way stop and suddenly noticed the van in front of me. The license plate read: HE HEARS. All the anxiety melted away. God's peace settled upon me as my confidence in His ability to solve the problem replaced my fretting.

In contrast, circumstances can mislead. My daughter finished college a few weeks ago and is looking for work. She began to notice commercials about a halfway house advertising jobs for case managers. Although she had no desire to work there, she wondered if God was trying to tell her something. So we prayed that God would either give her a desire for that type of employment if that was His will, or redirect her thoughts and give her no peace about applying.

Thoughts of the position disappeared immediately, confirming that God has other plans for her.

These are just a few common ways that God speaks to us. Again, there is no limit to His creativity. He may use foreign words or the five senses to communicate. There are so many nuances to hearing God that cannot be covered in this book. Please take the time to read more extensively on this subject. Although no one hears perfectly, it is vital to learn how to hear as accurately as possible. Check out Larry Kreider's books *Speak, Lord, I'm Listening* and *Hearing God 30 Different Ways*. (See appendix C for additional resources.)

Lies and Deceptions That Block Us

God created His children for intimate friendship with Him. Friendships are two-way streets, not cul-de-sacs where we do all the talking and He does all the listening. Satan has worked overtime to convince the Body of Christ that God does not communicate directly with people anymore. We need to dismantle the lies and deceptions that keep us from a close partnership with our Creator.

"God Speaks Only to Special People"

I believed this lie for twenty years. It never occurred to me that I might hear God speak until I attended a class based on Cindy Jacobs' book *The Voice of God*. I heard the testimony of a young man who was hearing God talk to him before he even got saved. Imagine that! But God did the same thing with the apostle Paul before his conversion. The teachers of the class were ordinary people, but they were hearing God on a regular basis. Why not me? Why not you?

As His children, we are all special in His sight. Jesus even calls us His friends (see John 15:15). To be a friend of Jesus makes us uniquely special. I am no more qualified to hear from God than you. It is simply a matter of training and practice.

"I Am Not Spiritual Enough"

We all start off on the same foot spiritually and take one step at a time toward God. The more time you spend seeking God through reading the Bible, praying and listening, the more chances you will have to hear God because you are correctly positioned to receive. Whether you are a new believer or have been saved for thirty years, you are spiritual enough right now to hear from God.

"God Doesn't Care about the Small Stuff"

All of creation screams, *Details, details!* Think about quantum physics or the human genome. Each is full of details. If God did not care about the small stuff, why did He create hundreds of thousands of species of butterflies, insects and creepy crawly things? There are thousands of species of bacteria alone—you cannot get much smaller than that. He even numbers the hairs on our heads.

The Bible tells us that God knows when each sparrow falls (see Matthew 10:29). Why does He keep track of millions of sparrows all over the planet if He does not care about the small stuff in our lives? Jesus assures us that God provides for the birds, then asks, "Are you not much more valuable than they?" (Matthew 6:26). I have not come across any verses in the Bible that tell us to limit our prayers based on size, weight, cost or time. Does God always give me details? No, many times He gives me just enough information to take the next step. But it never hurts to ask.

"God Doesn't Speak to Believers Anymore"

As discussed in chapter 1, many churches teach that God stopped speaking once the Bible was completed or the last apostle died. The New Testament confirms, however, that God continues to communicate with us (see John 14:16). That is what I told the woman at the end of my Bible study that day: "Yes, God does speak to us today." To my relief she did not call in a firing squad. I found that the other class members were equally curious.

God created us for relationship with Him. What healthy relationship does not include back-and-forth communication? Could it be that the enemy of our souls has deceived us into thinking God does not care or has no time to talk to us?

"It's Too Hard"

Sometimes when I share stories of God intersecting various aspects of my life, I sense that others are interested, but they doubt that they have what it takes to go from where they are to hearing God on a regular basis. It seems too hard; it will take too much time, and time is in short supply. Yet if someone told them that they could receive answers to all their problems, counseling when times are tough, a lifetime supply of food, clothing and all the necessities of life (plus some extras) with peace and joy thrown in, they would jump at the chance.

If we found time to learn how to ride a bicycle or drive a car, can we make the effort to learn to hear God? The end results are so spectacular, who would not want to invest time each day listening to Him? Decision making becomes easier as we learn to access God's divine wisdom. The time and stress saved in the long run more than make up for what is spent in the initial stages of developing a more intimate relationship with Him. It is not only worth the effort, it is fun! If you can sit on a couch and watch a half-hour sitcom, you can sit on the same couch and spend time listening to God. Which is more eternally significant?

Now that we understand God wants to be in partnership with us, we are ready to look at the seven secrets to power praying—the predominant ways that we can access His wisdom. God is waiting to work miracles in our lives every day. Let's look at what you need to know about how it is done.

Remember . . .

- You can learn to listen expectantly, without putting limits on how God will speak to you.
- God's promises are conditional on faith and obedience.
- The Lord wants to communicate His heart and His wisdom to you on a regular basis.
- Are you expecting and positioning yourself to hear personalized answers to your prayers?

PART 2

Applying
the 7 Secrets *to*
Power Praying

5

Secret #1:
Say Yes First

Life seems to keep handing us problems that defy our natural intelligence and human reasoning. Early in my dermatology residency one professor advised me that the best thing to pray for is wisdom. From that day on I prayed for God's wisdom and a teachable heart. I certainly needed it. Was it my imagination or did the toughest cases seem to appear on my watch? It was a decisive moment on my spiritual time line, one that would eventually bear much fruit. No matter what we are praying for, God in His infinite wisdom has an answer. His solutions will top anything that we could generate on our own.

The first secret to power praying—to say yes first—has to do with obedience to His will. Like the servant in the parable of the talents, if I am obedient in what I have been given, God will trust me with more. In other words, if God knows that I am committed up front to obeying whatever He asks of me, He will entrust me with more of His wisdom. If my heart is double-minded, however, and I ask for help with a problem, the answer may be delayed until I am ready to embrace His will in that matter. Saying yes first is a prerequisite to the fast track that accesses God's wisdom. Here is how I learned it.

"Can we go to the bookstore?" My son is a voracious reader, and even as a youngster he loved to visit bookstores.

"Only if you're doing the buying," I replied. Reading is my passion, too, but we had stacks of unshelved books at home. That was not something I needed to spend any more money on. While Mark browsed, I sequestered myself in the car until the chilly autumn day forced me into the warmth of the store with this declaration to the Lord: *I am not buying any more books! I have enough already.*

That "prayer" was meant to keep cash from flying out of my wallet. As Mark finished shopping I purposely averted my eyes from the tempting book covers. If I did not look, I would not buy. An odd sensation suddenly enveloped my body from head to toe, intensifying until my feet felt riveted to the carpet. Mark noticed the strange look on my face.

"Mom, are you okay?"

My answer surprised both of us. "The presence of the Lord is so strong I'm pinned to this spot," I said. "I can't move." This was a first. What in the world was God doing? I had no idea that I was one step away from a life-changing book. I glanced at the shelf next to me. *Experiencing the Spirit* by Henry and Melvin Blackaby caught my eye.

Lord, I don't need another book. . . .

My feet were paralyzed. I picked up the book, opened it randomly and asked the Lord, *Do You want me to buy this book?*

Buy it for Sally, He said, *but you read it first.* Standing there, I read a few pages, and the Lord embossed the content onto my spirit. My only chance to exit the store would be to obey. I *had* to buy this book. The paralysis lifted as soon as I made that decision.

Experiencing the Spirit brought a life-altering conviction to my soul: If Christ is Lord of my life, then the answer to *anything* God asks should be yes, even before knowing His requests. As Richard Stearns, president of World Vision United States, says in his book *The Hole in Our Gospel*, once we decide Christ is really Lord of our lives, then none of His requests is optional.

Why is such a simple concept so hard to follow? Because His ways and thoughts are higher than ours. We simply cannot understand everything He asks us to do. It requires faith. It requires trusting in His character—He is always good, He is always righteous in all He does and He wants His best for us. We can learn that only through experience, by saying yes to every request. *Every* no is a missed opportunity to know the Lord on a deeper level, to learn to trust Him in all things and to receive His richest blessings. With every no we shoot ourselves in the foot.

A friend invited me to a prayer group concerning state and national issues, especially an anti-abortion bill that was coming up for vote. My intense aversion to politics would have prompted an automatic no to the invitation. But after reading the Blackaby book I decided to pray about it.

"Lord, I hate politics, but I'll say yes to this invitation if it's what You want me to do." I sat and waited. Then I realized that someday I would meet those aborted babies in heaven. Which would I say to them: that I tried to stop the abortions or that I ignored their plight? A peaceful conviction (not guilt or condemnation) accompanied these thoughts. No longer could I ignore political issues. In a few minutes God connected my heart to this assignment. Week after week we prayed for the unborn and for state and national leaders. Several times we drove to the state capitol and prayed at the Statehouse. God used this experience to change my heart about political involvement and praying for political issues.

What a privilege to be asked by the Creator of the universe to do something for Him! Yet how many times, instead of being honored, humbled and excited to see what He will do through us, do we moan and complain? I know because I struggle with this. "Oh, God, please don't ask me to . . ." If we imprinted on the forefront of our minds that God empowers us and qualifies us for every task through His Holy Spirit, perhaps we would enjoy His divine directions more instead of focusing on our weaknesses and complaining.

When we contemplate saying yes to God *before* He reveals His will to us, we stand at the crossroads of belief and unbelief. Are we confident that He wants the finest for us and is trustworthy no matter what our circumstances look like? Or do we amble down the road of unbelief—"This doesn't make sense. I don't trust Him. I'd better do it myself." This is the critical test of whether faith in the Lord is merely head knowledge or the foundation on which we base all of our decisions. Power praying entails fully embracing God's will and giving Him the final say in our decisions.

If our knowledge of Scripture is not anchored to commitment and rooted in a personal relationship with the Lord, our minds will overflow with facts from reading the Bible, studying theology or attending church, but our prayers will be susceptible to hijacking by doubt, deception, fear, anxiety or discouragement. Without the underpinning of an intimate relationship with the Lord and dependence on the Holy Spirit for guidance, we can end up confused and unsure of how to pray.

The Pharisees knew the Scriptures, but Jesus told them, "You study the Scriptures diligently because you think that in them you have eternal life. These are the very Scriptures that testify about me, yet you refuse to come to me to have life" (John 5:39–40). Mere head knowledge can lead us into error if we rely on our limited human reasoning for decisions and then ask God to bless them. Scripture warns us, "Woe to those who are wise in their own eyes and clever in their own sight!" (Isaiah 5:21).

Beliefs rooted in the heart, however, that are married to the truth in Scripture, enable us to put it all on the line for the Lord with absolute assurance that He is our ultimate source of wisdom, provision and power. Faith looks at the problem, knows with *certainty* that God will release the answer and removes the stress from decision making. The Lord promises: "If any of you lacks wisdom, you should ask God, who gives generously to all without finding fault, and it will be given to you" (James 1:5). He is waiting for us to ask and to listen.

The only condition of our asking is that we must ask in faith (see James 1:6). Faith resides in the heart, not the head. Faith is absolute confidence that God means what He says. Why rely on our limited thinking when He promises to give wisdom liberally?

When stressed, I picture Jesus asleep in the boat with the disciples while the wind kicks up waves and threatens to capsize their vessel (see Mark 4:35–41). I imagine my head on a pillow next to His. He is not worried one bit. Jesus has perfect peace because He has the perfect solution, and He wants us to experience His peace in our storms, too. No matter what is happening in our lives, He is ready to solve our problems.

As we practice saying yes first, we may find ourselves hesitating. When an offering is being taken at church and we ask how much He wants us to give, what if He names an amount that makes us choke? Is He Lord of our finances? Completely? Often money issues test the reality of His lordship in our lives. If we give that sacrificial gift, will He provide for our tomorrows? Can we say yes to God when the journey is different from what we expected or wanted, or when His request pulls us out of our comfort zones?

Amelia dreamed of working with Rolland and Heidi Baker, founders and directors of Iris Ministries. Two years ago she raised the finances and signed up for a ten-day mission trip to join them in Mozambique. On the day of her departure, Amelia and I arrived at the airport at 5:30 a.m. Standing in line to check her bag we saw the word *canceled* next to her flight number. How could this be happening on the very first leg when we had bathed this trip in prayer and had peace it was God's will? She had to be in Washington, D.C., by 10:30 a.m. in order to meet her traveling group.

My prayers kicked into overdrive as I petitioned God to help Amelia meet her group on time. As we waited in the line to talk with an agent, out from a back room came a young man, yawning, and looking no more than eighteen years old. *Lord, not him! He doesn't look old enough to be an agent. Please give us the one with the gray hair!* My hopes plummeted as the senior agent took the woman in front of us and the sleepy lad motioned us forward. His best reticketing offer included a 2:30 p.m. flight to Washington and an overnight stay in Ethiopia—she would be traveling three days *alone* before reaching Mozambique. My response? There was no way our attractive college-aged daughter would be staying alone overnight in Ethiopia. He needed to come up with a better plan.

On the verge of canceling the whole trip, I turned to my daughter and asked, "Do you still want to go?" She responded calmly that it was God's will and she was going. "Then you wait here. I have to pray." Finding a quiet spot about ten feet away I implored God. *This is crazy. I can't let her travel all by herself to Africa. Oh, God, help me! If You still want her to go, I say yes, but I can't do this. I just can't do this.*

Let her go. God's gentle response was not the answer I desperately hoped for. *Let her go.* I wanted a paragraph's worth of assurance that a special contingent of super angels was being assigned, that He would get her to Washington miraculously, or that the rest of the group would be delayed, too, so that she could travel with her team. *Let her go* ran through my head over and over. It was the greatest crisis of belief and obedience I had ever faced. But I said yes.

By the time I returned, the ticket agent had rebooked her through Europe then Kenya, Tanzania and finally on to Mozambique. Later that day as I watched Amelia go through security it was all I could do not to pull her out of line and take her home. As soon as she was out of sight I ducked into the restroom behind me and sobbed my heart out in one of the stalls.

My prayers were not answered the way I would have liked; however, Amelia reached Mozambique safe and sound after even more delayed flights and rebookings. Through that experience we learned on a much deeper level how faithful God is.

Yes is the fastest way to receiving God's best, but be prepared for times of testing. You may even feel, as I did that day, that you have been tossed into a fiery furnace heated seven times hotter than anything you have ever endured (see Daniel 3:19–20). But Jesus will be right there with you.

When belief is interwoven with faith, the two become the foundation that stabilizes our lives. Jesus declared that when we build our houses (our lives) on the rock, the storms of life will not destroy us (see Matthew 7:24–27). When we take the risk of saying yes first, we will find that He is absolutely trustworthy and that His ways are indeed higher and better than ours (see Isaiah 55:9).

It may feel like bungee jumping off a tall bridge, but He will not let go of the cord. It is well worth some discomfort to grow your faith and your confidence in God as you pray. His answers will amaze you. He will reveal solutions that you would never think of. Your small steps of obedience now will enable you to handle anything that comes your way later in life.

Yes to the Lord means no strings attached and no bargaining. I was shocked the first time I read Joy Dawson's book *Intimacy with God*, in which she states that delayed obedience is disobedience. I put the book down immediately after reading that. Was she serious? Was that true? Goodness, there were countless times that I dragged my feet and my attitude before finally complying with what God wanted me to do. A deep sense of repentance came over me. I was only thinking of my side of the equation, not His. My "Yes, but" had strings attached, and I was holding the strings, not God. Was He really Lord of my entire life—Lord of my time, my resources and my talents? If our hearts are truly anchored in Him, then yes is the only answer.

Ruth's relationship to her mother-in-law illustrates this principle. After Ruth's husband died, she insisted on following Naomi to her home country, which was foreign to Ruth (see Ruth 1:16–17). She left her family of origin, friends and culture to embrace Naomi's. Can we, like Ruth, say yes to God's plan even when it seems foreign and we have no idea what to expect? Abraham (see Genesis 12:1), Isaac (see Genesis 22:9) and Esther (see Esther 4:16) all said yes before they knew what God would eventually do. Like Ruth, they experienced God's faithful provision.

One morning, while waiting in my car for our high school moms' prayer group to begin, the thought popped into my head to go to a restaurant several blocks from the school. Not being hungry, I dismissed the idea. It recurred. I ignored it again and again until it occurred to me that perhaps God was behind this thought. "Lord, if this is You, please bring this up again, but if not, please erase this thought from my mind. I'm not hungry." The thought returned. *Maybe God wants me to run into someone there. I'd better go in case this is really from Him.*

Within minutes I pulled into a parking space and turned to get my purse off the backseat. No purse. The backseat was empty. The sinking feeling of having driven without my license was quickly replaced with the unsettling thought that I had misheard God. "Lord, if that was You, would You help me understand why You sent me here when You knew I had no money?" I grabbed the Amplified Bible lying next to me and randomly opened to Isaiah 55, hoping that God would clear up this mystery. My eyes fell on the first verse:

Wait and listen, everyone who is thirsty! Come to the waters; and he who has no money, come, buy and eat! Yes, come, buy [priceless, spiritual] wine and milk without money and without price [simply for the self-surrender that accepts the blessing].

God had dropped me right into the middle of an object lesson. Minutes later I shared that lesson with my prayer group. All the spiritual food and drink we could ever want is available simply by surrendering to Him and accepting the blessings that come with that surrender. Saying yes did not cost me a penny, but I learned something priceless.

When I find myself struggling with saying yes, I review His character. He is all wise, all knowing, all powerful and all present. I will start praising Him for His might, His faithfulness, His unconditional love and His protection. As I praise and thank Him for these attributes, my faith increases. My thoughts shift from my concerns to His provision.

If you are uncertain whether or not you can say yes first, ask yourself these questions:

Is anything too hard for God?

Is there any problem He cannot and does not want to fix in my life?

Is there anything God does not know about my situation?

Is God wise enough to come up with the best solution?

Is God *really* worried about this problem?

Does He have enough resources to provide for my needs?

As you build a history of trusting God in the smaller matters, you will find it easier to say yes in the larger ones. God gave me many experiences of being stretched out of my comfort zone, building my faith and trust in Him, to prepare me for the Mozambique experience. He knows your level of faith and how to grow it one step at a time.

What if you just cannot bring yourself to say yes even once? God appreciates your honesty. He knows you are struggling. What did Jesus say? "The spirit is willing, but the flesh is weak" (Matthew 26:41). I have a solution. It is Secret #2: Give God your password.

Remember . . .

- Praying for wisdom and a teachable heart are the two best prayers you can pray.
- If Christ is your Lord, then yes is the answer He is looking for.
- Yes is the fastest way to receive God's best, but be prepared for times of testing.
- Do you want to risk shooting yourself in the foot by saying no?

6

Secret #2:
Give God Your Password

It was a sultry Sunday afternoon—perfect for putting my feet up and immersing myself in a book. After all, it was a day of rest. What possessed our children to pick that day to use our free tickets for a professional baseball game? Coupled with their request came tormenting thoughts of sweating for hours under a cruel, cloudless sky while feigning interest in a small leather-covered ball.

No way. This is Mom's day off. Nothing will budge me! Nothing. I mustered enough maturity to turn down their appeal without whining pitifully. Then my son, who was ten at the time, struck a blow below the belt. "Would you pray about it?" How dare he use my own strategy against me!

Could I possibly refuse his request and maintain any form of spiritual integrity after teaching both of my children to pray about everything? The intensity of my reaction to the steamy weather precluded my having an open mind. In fact, I had no idea how to pray. I knew with certainty that anything I heard would echo my desires and not reflect God's heart. Feeling cornered and desperate, I handed it all over to God, lump sum.

"God, in the worst possible way I do not want to go to a ball game today. I hate heat and humidity. More than anything I want to stay home and read a book, but I give You permission to change my heart and mind about this if You want me to go." It was the only thing that came to mind. Forcing myself not to think about the comforting caress of the armchair, I headed upstairs to change my church clothes and to divert my thoughts from both the ball game and the book. I determined not to talk myself in or out of a decision. Since I secretly believe God has special compassion for stressed-out moms, surely He would take pity on me and allow me to stay home.

To my complete surprise, within twenty minutes every trace of negativity evaporated, replaced by genuine excitement about going to the game. How did God do that? No mystical moment with Him or Fatherly rebuke about spending the afternoon with the family had entered my thoughts. The effortless transformation of my emotions totally baffled me, but delighted Tom and the kids. Off we drove to the ballpark. Even more surprising, our seats were nestled in the shade for most of the afternoon. Was it my imagination, or did the hot dogs taste especially first-rate? To this day it is a special memory among our family outings.

My experience that Sunday was another spiritual serendipity. My determination to stay home, though not a sin, was blocking my ability to see God's best for our family. Handing

Him the "password" to my thoughts and emotions—that is, giving God permission to change my heart and mind—was a new concept for me. It allowed Him to determine the outcome of that decision with minimal effort on my part. He simply transformed my attitude supernaturally. It felt as though He had vaccinated me against a bad mood without my feeling the prick of a needle. I would have missed those cherished memories at the ballpark by my unwillingness to embrace His better plan.

When distractions or strong desires prevent you from applying the first secret to power praying—saying yes to God willingly out of obedience—the solution is to give God your password. It sounds something like this: "Lord, I give you permission to change my mind and my emotions. I want Your best in this matter." Give any fear, doubt or anxiety to God and ask Him to replace it with His peace. Relax and rest for a while in His presence. If you are too distraught, busy yourself with something routine like mowing the lawn, cooking or cleaning, to take your mind off your problem. Revisit the issue in prayer when peace is reestablished.

Giving God the password to our souls (minds, wills and emotions) enables us to receive the mind of Christ—which is tranquil, confident and uncluttered with worry. It removes those things that block us from His provision of wisdom, joy and peace. Is the God who fed five thousand men (plus women and children) with five loaves of bread and two fish worried about supplying our needs? The Israelites did not eat just a bite-sized morsel; they were filled. He even made sure there were twelve baskets of leftovers (see Matthew 14:19–21). His abundant provision is still available today, whether we are praying for food, finances or wisdom. Giving God our password is a painless means to regaining peace and joy and to making wise choices.

"Peace I leave with you; my peace I give you. I do not give to you as the world gives. Do not let your hearts be troubled and do not be afraid" (John 14:27). The Lord's peace cannot be purchased. It results from centering our lives on His plans and purposes. Having lived much of my life without it, I now treasure the mental and emotional tranquility that comes supernaturally when my mind and heart are in sync with His.

Several years ago my friend Diana called with free tickets to visit a new museum. Although I love museums, for some reason this one held no appeal for me. So I immediately said no thanks. While I was declining her gracious invitation, the Lord was simultaneously telling me to accept. Unable to override my disinterest, though, I held firm. Then Diana asked if I would pray about it. I hung up the phone and prayed reluctantly: "Lord, I really have no interest in this particular museum. If You want me to go, please change my heart and mind." It took less than two minutes for me to dial her back and accept with excitement. I had to laugh at Diana's response.

"The Lord told me to invite you, but I didn't want to say that."

"Diana," I said, "if you had said that, it would have saved us both another phone call!" But God had His reason for keeping her silent. He needed to deal with my predetermination not to go. Giving God the password to my emotions saved time and put me in the center of His will. I did not have to spend hours wrestling with negative feelings. I gave Him the key to alter my attitude, and He did. I so thoroughly enjoyed that museum that I am a repeat visitor.

Giving God the password to our thoughts and hearts gives us, in turn, the passkey to His will. Many have missed wonderful blessings simply because they "didn't feel like it." That feeling is a red flag to me that God may have something great in store that Satan wants me to miss. God has plans and blessings for each day. It pays to pray.

There are many unexpected benefits of giving God the password to my mind, will and emotions. When grocery shopping, for instance, I spend a few seconds before getting out of the car asking God to put a check in my spirit so that I do not buy anything unnecessary. I might pick up an item that is not on my list and feel a tugging at my spirit or hear the inner voice of the Lord say, *You don't really need that.* When I put the item back, peace returns. By intentionally giving God permission to change us, we are assured that He will redirect our steps when necessary. Being in the center of His will releases peace and security that money cannot buy.

God has some secrets, too. Have you ever wondered what is on God's heart—and how knowing what is there helps you pray with power? That is our next topic.

Remember . . .

- You can short-circuit negative attitudes by asking God to change your heart and mind.
- Peace comes supernaturally when your mind and heart are in sync with His.
- Giving God the password to your thoughts and emotions unlocks the passkey to His will.
- Is your life centered on His plans and purposes? If not, will you give Him your password?

7

Secret #3:
Tap into God's Heart

Your mother will not die this year.

What? Why was God telling me that?

Your mother will not die this year. God's declaration came to me yet a third time, quietly in my head, but distinctly the voice I had come to recognize over the past sixteen years as the Lord's. I recorded the sentence in my journal.

My friend Suelee had invited me to her home that day to pray about a personal concern. We began by asking God what was on His heart. In the stillness of listening, the Lord made that pronouncement about my mother. She was 88 years old, very active and in good health, but for some reason thoughts about losing her had begun to ransack my mind. As I pondered God's unexpected proclamation, tranquility edged out the anxiety. How gracious of the Lord to reassure me and lift that burden without my even asking! Little did I know how important that information would be three months later.

On August 12, 2011, a police officer phoned our home at 4:45 a.m. to report that an ambulance was transporting my mother to a local hospital. At nine o'clock the previous evening, she had fallen while stepping from her house into the garage, fracturing her pelvis in three places and breaking her shoulder. Her only hope of rescue was to drag herself the full length of the garage to the open door. Bone cold from the unseasonably chilly 53-degree temperature, she lay shivering on the concrete for seven hours, before a neighbor heard her shouting, "Call 911!"

We rushed to the hospital. The emergency room doctor guided us through the facts. My mother needed three pints of blood and multiple doses of morphine to temper the severe pain. Since that facility was not equipped to handle major trauma, he had arranged to transport her to a level-one trauma center, where an orthopedic doctor specializing in pelvic fractures would evaluate her. At that point the ER doc's tone took an abrupt turn as he pulled up her X rays.

"Just the pelvic fractures would be bad enough, but you add in the compression of her pelvis and the fractured shoulder and the prognosis is not good. I recommend you call in your family members. There's a good chance she might not make it." Although the X rays were painful to look at, the black-and-white "facts" were no match for God's truth.

I mustered a smile and replied, "No, she'll be fine." It was clear why God had prepared me for this moment: My words had to agree with the declaration of God's heart on this matter three months earlier.

By the time we reached the next hospital, another ER physician had already obtained a second set of X rays. The petite

Asian doctor repeated almost word for word what the first physician had stated. She told me that her own grandfather had died three months after a similar accident and that I needed to call the family in and prepare them.

"She'll be fine," I said firmly. What did it matter if this doctor thought I was crazy or in serious denial? I knew that without faith it is impossible to please God (see Hebrews 11:6). Faith is the conviction and expectation that God's promise will manifest in due time (see Hebrews 11:1). What was about to follow would try that faith, but I was willing to pay the price to see God's miracle. My job was to "watch, stand fast in the faith, be brave, be strong" (1 Corinthians 16:13 NKJV).

Medical complications did indeed challenge my reliance on God's declaration. My mother developed atrial fibrillation (a rapid, irregular heartbeat) and was admitted to the ICU; her blood pressure dropped dangerously low; she developed symptoms of pneumonia; and the doctors-in-training planned to discharge her before she was medically stable. With each setback I retreated to the lounge at the end of the hallway to affirm God's heart on the matter. I prayed for godly wisdom and declared that she would not die, but live, to the glory of God (see Psalm 118:17).

Two exhausting months later my mother returned to her own home, walking without assistance. With additional out-patient rehab she took up her former activities—book clubs, card clubs and gardening.

I learned this secret of tapping into God's heart in a prayer group for moms of high schoolers. It seemed at first as though our lists of concerns took more time than our prayers. Sometimes we left just as anxious as when we came in. One day someone suggested that since God already knew what troubled us, why not just praise and thank Him for who He is and for the answers that He would provide? That shifted our focus from the problems to the Problem Solver. It enabled us to see God, not as a vendor of favors, but as One to be revered and lifted up, One who would share His heart with us.

By the time Mark was a sophomore in high school our prayer group was routinely listening for what God wanted us to pray. We released personal burdens to the Lord silently at the beginning of the prayer time so that our hearts and minds were free from distractions and worries. That enabled us to focus on God's heart for the school and for our families. It amazed us to hear one person pray and then discover that others had heard the same thing from God. How exciting to experience His personal touch on each of our lives! Our faith deepened. We sensed His presence as we prayed what was on His heart. After listening and praying through what the Lord showed us, we addressed any personal requests. We left full of peace instead of burdened.

"This is the confidence we have in approaching God: that if we ask anything according to his will, he hears us. And if we know that he hears us—whatever we ask—we know that we have what we asked of him" (1 John 5:14–15). Secret #3, tapping into God's heart, guarantees answers to our prayers. When we pray God's will, we receive the answers to our petitions.

How do we know God's will? We find out what is on His heart. When my mom wanted to give up, I encouraged her with confidence. Knowing God's will influenced every decision I made about her care.

Just this past spring Amelia needed two internships to complete her degree in psychology. The department had only three choices for her first internship—two overseas and one stateside. Amelia had an impression to apply to the one in Colorado, and although she did not meet one of the requirements to qualify for that program, she applied regardless. As we waited I wondered, *What will she do if they don't accept her?*

During prayer one day I asked God what was on His heart. *Amelia will be accepted*, He said. That comforting inner voice melted away all concern about her application. From that point on, I thanked Him for His promise. Weeks later her acceptance notice arrived with an added bonus—a partial scholarship that she had not even applied for! We rejoiced at God's miraculous provision.

Why is tapping into God's heart so important? Jesus commands us to seek first God's Kingdom and His righteousness and our needs will be met (see Matthew 6:33). How many times have we failed to put God first because we are focused on our own agendas? Are we giving priority to social media and the Internet rather than the Lord? The busyness of family life and work can relegate God to the background of our lives. Romans 8:5 states that believers are to "set their minds on and seek those things which gratify the [Holy] Spirit" (AMPLIFIED). What gratifies God's Spirit? Could it be focusing primarily on Him and not ourselves?

When we think deeply about our place here on earth, are we mindful that we are here at God's invitation, that it is He who provides everything for us? Jesus said, "Apart from me you can do nothing" (John 15:5). He gives us breath, and He is able to take it away. It is by God's grace that we have income, food on the table and clothes on our backs. He deserves first place in our thoughts and decisions.

"However, when He, the Spirit of truth, has come, He will *guide you* into all truth; for He will not speak on His own authority, but *whatever He hears He will speak*; and He will *tell you things to come*" (John 16:13 NKJV, emphasis added). And how do we receive those divine downloads? We spend time listening to God.

Think about it: We make time to check our cell phones numerous times a day to see if we have missed a call. Are we as diligent about seeing if God has anything to say to us each day? If every prayer consists of a list of our needs followed by a quick amen, when does the Holy Spirit have a chance to give us the messages that Jesus promised He would send directly from the Father? We have to give God our full attention by purposefully letting go of the microphone and handing it to Him. We cannot do all the talking and expect to know God's heart.

Whenever I pray, my goal is to ask God what is on His heart before I ask about my concerns. Sometimes He assures me of safety for an upcoming trip or provision for our needs. Sometimes He gives facts beyond my realm of knowing, like telling me my mother would not die that year. He may impart knowledge that I need in order to make wise choices. At other times I ask and hear silence. That is fine, too. At least I know I am not missing a vital piece of information for lack of asking.

Nothing excites me more than hearing from God. My faith soars during those encounters. Who would not want to sit down and hear from the God of the universe? There must be a reason that God gave every believer in Christ His

Holy Spirit. How else can He declare to us the "things that are to come"?

Paul advises: "Set your minds and *keep them set on what is above* (the higher things), not on the things that are on the earth" (Colossians 3:2 AMPLIFIED, emphasis added). Setting our minds on the higher things takes commitment and effort. It also means that we need to relinquish some of the standard means of decision making; in particular, discarding our pros and cons lists. Let me show you what I mean.

Remember . . .

- Pray with a focus on the Problem Solver, not the problem.
- To pray God's will, ask what is on His heart.
- Seek to gratify God's Holy Spirit by focusing primarily on Him, not yourself.
- Is anything crowding God out of first place in your life?

8

Secret #4:
Toss the Pros and Cons List

C-R-A-Z-Y—I could almost feel the letters being etched on my forehead the first time I spoke to our middle school prayer group. The moms sitting around the conference room table were expecting a super-spiritual teaching. Instead, God had directed me to talk about tossing our pros and cons lists into the trash. I felt sure somebody at that table would think I was nuts.

My lead-off Scripture was Romans 8:6: "Now the mind of the flesh [which is sense and reason without the Holy Spirit] is death" (AMPLIFIED). As I mentioned in chapter 3, the blunt force of those words had compelled me to reckon with God's truth regarding human logic and reasoning. Our minds need to be saturated with God's Spirit. I set about trying to explain that concept, fully aware that our culture places high value on intellect and self-reliance.

It was years later before one of the women admitted to me, "When you spoke at that prayer meeting that day, I thought you were crazy. But now I see what you mean." She had a teachable heart and was willing to be stretched. Are you open to trying something new, a secret to praying with power that will usher in amazing answers to prayer?

Before I discovered this secret, it was second nature for me to take a sheet of paper and list the advantages and disadvantages when making a decision. I loved making lists. They were concrete, something I could see in the natural, just like rashes and warts—which is one reason I chose dermatology as a profession. I distinctly remember poring over pros and cons lists in high school. It developed into quite a science for me, because the length of each list was not always the determining factor. One emotionally laden item in the pros column might be worth two in the cons column. And suppose both had the exact same number of items, neither of which was persuasive enough to help me cast a deciding vote? It never occurred to me to pray and ask God what the best choice was. My prayers back then were mostly monologues.

Depending on anyone else—including God—to make my decisions felt about as safe as skidding down an icy mountain road with no guardrail. By generically asking God for wisdom, but never really seeking or listening for His *specific* answers, I was actually tying His hands behind His back while I relied on "self" for all decisions. Romans 8:6 changed that. Through trial and error I learned to trust that His ways are infinitely better than mine.

In its broadest sense, Secret #4 is about more than tossing away our pros and cons lists. It is about laying down our need to have every decision make sense. No way could God have used me to march around Jericho, build an ark or fight along with Gideon when I was in my teens! I made most of my decisions by weighing data and analyzing solutions. God gave me a brain; I used it, but God did not really figure into my choices. I ran on my own wisdom and strength.

Postgraduate education simply reinforced my self-reliance. A semester of law school entrenched my linear way of finding solutions. Nine years of medical training and eight years of private practice honed my decision-making skills as a physician but were useless when it came to making decisions with God at the center. I mentioned in chapter 2 how God told me to quit my medical practice at what seemed like the worst possible time . . . my husband out of work . . . the malpractice suit.

For several months I wrestled with God over my career. My cons list was extensive. We would lose our health and dental insurance and 90 percent of our income. Quitting might adversely affect my lawsuit if I needed one of my partners to testify on my behalf. Shelving my medical skills might make it difficult to reenter the field. I would be back to pinching pennies, something I had grown weary of during my younger years. And how in the world would I keep my sanity without work?

Regarding the pros list—well, to be honest I could not see anything positive about quitting work. It made no sense. In my mind it meant financial and professional disaster.

Finally it came down to hearing God and choosing to obey. If this was truly God's idea, I had to let the list go. God patiently led me through prayer, wise counsel and eventually an abiding conviction that yes, indeed, He wanted me at home.

What if spouses disagree on a decision? Ask the Lord for unity in the decision-making process. If both are willing to lay down their opinions, commit to seeking God's best solution and give Him the password to their thoughts and emotions, the Lord will bring agreement in the decision as they continue to seek His will.

Paul urges us to throw away arguments and anything that stands against the knowledge of God and to intentionally center our thoughts on obedience to Christ (see 2 Corinthians 10:5). In other words, I wanted control of solutions, but God wanted me to master my thoughts by submitting them to His authority and refusing those that provoked anxiety.

We need the mind of Christ, but how do we acquire it, and what does it look like? The Bible is full of spiritual wisdom but does not tell us specifics—such as which apartment to rent or how much to spend on a vacation.

We acquire this skill, quite simply, by listening. We must come to terms with our limitations, admit our need for God and include Him in every part of our lives. Granted, learning to do this does not happen overnight. It took time for me to learn how to put aside my beloved pros and cons lists and wait for Him to speak. Romans 8:6 challenged me, but it brought exciting results. Sometimes the answers came to me while I sat and listened. Many times the solutions popped into my mind later as I did something routine like cooking or driving. In time I learned to trust that I was hearing His voice—even when it made no sense initially.

In 2 Kings 4:1–7 we read that a creditor was about to enslave a widow's two sons in order to pay off her debt. Elisha asked what she had in her house: just one jar of oil. He told her to borrow as many jars as she could and pour the oil into them. As she obeyed, the oil multiplied and filled all of the borrowed jars, enabling the woman to sell the oil to pay her debt and spare her sons from imprisonment. That makes no sense in the natural. Nor does it make sense that ravens would bring bread and meat twice a day to feed Elijah (see 1 Kings 17:6) or that striking a rock with a rod would produce enough drinking water for millions of exiled Israelites in the desert (see Exodus 17:6).

Many times Christ's ministry did not make sense to the people around Him. He had no medical training, yet He healed everyone who came to Him. He was the Son of God, yet He violated "church" rules by healing on the Sabbath. He was not a chemist, yet He knew how to turn water to wine (see John 2:6–10). He was not a caterer, but He could feed thousands with one boy's lunch (see John 6:5–14).

Miracles do not make sense. If they did, they would not be supernatural manifestations of God's power. While His sense may seem like nonsense to us, listen to what Scripture says: "Do not deceive yourselves. If any of you think you are wise by the standards of this age, you should become 'fools' so that you may become wise. For the wisdom of this world is foolishness in God's sight" (1 Corinthians 3:18–19).

Are we willing to be fools for Christ? Do we really want to hinder God with our pros and cons lists and our logical thinking? Or do we want to give Him free rein to go above and beyond what we are capable of thinking and imagining with our natural abilities (see Ephesians 3:20)? Why limit His creativity? That is not to say that God never uses something we think of, but why restrict the Creator of the universe to only that which is within the bounds of human intelligence?

The following chart may help to clarify decision making.

	God	Human
Wisdom	Perfect	Imperfect
Provision	Abundant	Unreliable
Truth	Absolute	Partial
Knowledge	All knowing	Limited
Power	All powerful	Limited
Presence	Omnipresent	Limited

We can rely on our imperfect wisdom, limited knowledge and partial truth. Or we can submit our decisions to God who is all knowing, all powerful, all wise and the Author of all truth. Is there any question who will make the best decisions for *all* of our problems?

Ephesians 3:20–21 says: "Now to Him who is able to do exceedingly abundantly above all that we ask or think, according to the power that works in us, to Him be glory in the church by Christ Jesus" (NKJV). Ephesians 1:23 says further that the Church "is His body, the fullness of Him who fills all in all" (NKJV). Jesus lives within us by the presence of the Holy Spirit. Why not give Him carte blanche in every decision? He promises to do *abundantly above all* that we ask or imagine. If it is above what we can think or imagine, then only God can do it.

Jesus received all His directives from God the Father. Christ told His disciples that He could do nothing of His own accord but only what He saw His heavenly Father doing (see John 5:19). Notice that the disciples did not ask Jesus to teach them how to weigh the advantages and disadvantages, but how to pray (see Luke 11:1).

If you are still not convinced, note how the disciples chose a replacement for Judas. They did not sit down with résumés and debate the pros and cons of possible candidates. They committed the decision to the Lord, asking Him to show them through the casting of lots (see Acts 1:23–26). Again, the key is to commit our decisions to God and have Him confirm the correct answers.

To make wise decisions it helps to know all the details and what the future holds. There is only One who knows all of that. Are we going to the Source of all wisdom and knowledge for every decision? Romans 3:22 says that the righteousness of God "comes by believing with personal trust and confident reliance on Jesus Christ (the Messiah)" (AMPLIFIED). Are we *confidently* relying on the Lord or on ourselves?

When listening prayer is not taught in the home, we grow up learning to be self-sufficient and independent rather than humble and God-dependent. Part of teaching children to stand on their own two feet is to model kneeling before the Lord and admitting our total dependence upon Him. It is never too late to learn this. Why wait for a disaster or a personal crisis? Now is a great time to start.

God has cures for diseases waiting to be released to researchers who seek Him. He has creative solutions for businessmen and women, teachers and engineers. He has witty inventions stored up for those willing to pursue Him. He is the ultimate Problem Solver.

If you find that these secrets are too hard to implement in a situation you are facing right now, maybe it is time to "give up." How can you know when to give up in the natural and still be victorious in your prayer life? That is Secret #5.

Remember . . .

- Relying solely on human intellect and reasoning ties God's hands behind His back.
- God's ways are infinitely higher and superior to yours and might not make sense initially.
- To have the mind of Christ, release control of your circumstances and depend on the Holy Spirit for solutions.
- To experience supernatural answers to your prayers, are you willing to give God free rein in solving your problems?

9

Secret #5:
Know When to Give Up

I laid my head on the dining room table, too tired and emotionally depleted to begin writing my sophomore pathology paper. "Lord, I don't feel good. I'm exhausted. I just can't write this paper. Please write it through me." It was probably 90 percent complaint and 10 percent prayer. I felt incapable of stringing two intelligent sentences together, but an unyielding deadline loomed in the not too distant future, so I picked up my pen and began. I did not sense God's presence or power; there was no automatic handwriting. I simply did the next thing, having entrusted the entire process to Him.

Admitting defeat and surrendering to God made all the difference. To my great surprise the paper won a departmental award. Learning to give up when mentally and emotionally overwhelmed turned out to be an important secret to praying with power.

Many years later my young daughter threw herself across my bed wailing, "Mom, I can't remember these words." She tossed her spelling list at me like a white flag of surrender.

"That's great, sweetheart," I responded.

Before she could decide whether Mom was crazy or cruel, I quickly explained my thoughts. Memorizing was a monumental task for her. Since she was unable to do her assignment, I suggested she "give up," admit to God she could not do it and ask that He do it through her. She scampered off. About twenty minutes later Amelia marched in triumphantly, able to spell every word. We thanked God and gave Him the credit for what she could not do.

When we feel physically and emotionally unable to accomplish a task, we need to know how to give up and let God take over. This applies to studying for tests, applying for a job or dealing with difficult people, for example.

On my way to picking up the children after school one day, I was acutely aware of my frazzled nerves—not a good backdrop for dealing with tired children, preparing supper and helping with homework. As I pulled into the carpool line, I shot up a quick life-preserver prayer: "Lord, I have no patience right now. I simply cannot deal with the kids. Please be patient through me." As I laid my head on the pillow at the end of the day I suddenly realized how smoothly the entire afternoon and evening had unfolded. Peace and patience had pervaded our family. *God really answered that prayer. That's amazing. I'll have to try that again.* And so I did.

At social gatherings, for instance, if I felt unnerved by someone, I admitted my negative emotions and asked God to love that person through me. It was uncanny how I would forget about my irritation. At the end of the evening I found myself thinking, *I had a great time. God did it again!*

One day I had to remove a set of miniblinds from one of our kitchen windows. But no matter how hard I pushed and pulled on the top rail I could not release the blinds. In frustration I gave up. "God, I can't figure out how to take these blinds down. Would You help me?" As I sat and waited, a mental image directed me to one end of the blind with the impression to lift up a certain metal piece. That was the solution!

When I interviewed for my dermatology residency, I had no clue what the faculty might ask. I knew the competition would be stiff, with many more applicants than the two or three positions available. How could I stand out from the rest? I released it all to God: "When I open my mouth, please fill it with Your words." I found out later that the answers I gave in two very different interviews were exactly what those particular professors were looking for.

The Amplified translation of Matthew 7:7–8 instructs us to ask and keep on asking: "For everyone who keeps on asking receives." When I know what is on God's heart, I keep on asking, seeking and knocking.

So what determines when I "give up" and ask God to take over? When I have tried all I know to do or have exhausted my patience or willpower, before going into an emotional nose dive, I invite God to take over, do the task through me and restore my peace. Maintaining tranquility in our household is important, so I try to "give up" before anger sets in.

Is there a point at which I consider actually quitting? Yes, if I have asked God to take over yet still meet with continued failure, I will seek the Lord as to whether the assignment has changed or whether He is asking me to drop it. Since some tasks require the cooperation of others, if they are not responding to His plans, then at times God directs me to quit. At His direction I quit the task knowing that I have done all that He asked me to do. Warning signs that indicate it is too soon to quit include discouragement, doubt and distractions. If God has called you to do something, Scripture encourages us: "He who began a good work in you will carry it on to completion" (Philippians 1:6).

Now, I am not encouraging anyone to be passive or irresponsible, or to teach that to your family. As parents, we had to discern if our children were not putting forth their best efforts or if they were truly in over their heads. Allowing them to struggle to resolve their own problems had great value; we did not want to short-circuit their critical thinking. Teaching perseverance has high value in our home. But it was also important that they learn to partner with God. Jesus said, "With man this is impossible, but with God all things are possible" (Matthew 19:26 ESV). He also said, "If you can believe, all things are possible to him who believes" (Mark 9:23 NKJV). I wanted our kids to live lives full of faith and miracles.

Giving up is simply a way of admitting that we are out of ideas, out of our comfort zones or feeling unqualified for the situation, and that apart from Him we can do nothing. It is humbling to confess inadequacy. But Scripture promises us: "He guides the humble in what is right and teaches them his way" (Psalm 25:9). So acknowledging that we have truly come to the end of our abilities is not the end but the beginning of our dependence on God. It must be coupled with a teachable heart. Are we willing to admit defeat and listen to His wisdom?

We read in the Old Testament that King Jehoshaphat learned that the Moabites, the Ammonites and the Meunites planned to attack Judah. The odds were not in the Israelites' favor. The king and the people were terrified. All of Judah gathered together with the king to seek the Lord's help, and the king cried out to God: "We have no power to face this vast army that is attacking us. We do not know what to do, but our eyes are on you" (2 Chronicles 20:12).

King Jehoshaphat and the people knew they could not fight that battle, so they gave up. Then the Holy Spirit came upon one of the priests: "This is what the LORD says to you: 'Do not be afraid or discouraged because of this vast army. For the battle is not yours, but God's. . . . You will not have to fight this battle'" (verses 15, 17). The Lord delivered them miraculously: The enemy soldiers turned upon each other until not one was left alive. All the Israelites had to do was pick up the spoils.

Many times when I come to the end of myself I pray, "Lord, I don't know what to do, but my eyes are on You." Then I meditate on His many miracles. Focusing on what God has done in the past takes my mind off the problem and positions me to hear His solution.

God knows when we are completely out of resources. When we come to Him with humility and ask Him to work through us, He accomplishes what we cannot do in our own strength. Admitting our weaknesses shifts our reliance from our natural abilities to dependence on Him.

Have you ever prayed so hard that you were exasperated, weary and did not think you could pray one more word about your problem? Just thinking about it made your stomach grind? When I am at my wit's end, I write the issue on a scrap of paper, roll it up into a ball and then place it in a clay hand that I made to represent God's hand. As I do so, I recite Psalm 37:5: "Commit your way to the LORD, trust also in Him, and He shall bring it to pass" (NKJV).

That simple act of letting go lifts the burden off my shoulders. At that point I stop praying and thinking about the situation and trust that God has taken over. This idea came from Joy Dawson's book *The Fire of God*. She uses a small pillow to represent her problem and tosses the pillow away from her as she releases the issue to God. The pillow stays wherever it lands until she receives the answer to her prayer. Any unbreakable object can substitute for your prayer request. Toss it to God as you commit the problem to Him and trust He will act in His timing.

God's solutions always offset my inadequacies. Are they always miraculous? No, but they are always wise. There are times when I give up that God directs me to ask my husband for help or to call someone familiar with the problem. He may have me walk away and tackle the problem when I feel more refreshed. Or He may direct me to do something relaxing. Sometimes when I am engrossed in something else a solution pops into my head.

It helps to remember God's promise that we can do all things with Christ's help (see Philippians 4:13). The Amplified Bible states that He infuses strength into us. When we feel inadequate, helpless or weak, we can give up and lean on His strength, knowing that Christ within us is more than sufficient for our task.

For those times that we feel personally inadequate, we need to "give up" and look to God for the solution. But what about those frustrating times when we have direction from the Lord about His will for us, yet circumstances keep preventing us from moving forward? When this happens, God can show us how to open doors that appear to be padlocked. Let's see in the next chapter how this works.

Remember . . .

- When feeling totally inadequate to complete a task, it is time to release it to God and let Him take over.
- Admitting your weaknesses shifts your reliance on self to dependence on God.
- Christ within you is more than sufficient for your problems.
- When tempted to quit, why not ask God to do it through you?

10

Secret #6:
Open Locked Doors

One day as I was driving, a strong spiritual presence enveloped me. I pulled into a parking space, sensing that God had something important to share.

"What is it, Lord?"

How easy do you want Me to make things for you with your dad?

I knew God was referring to the situation my brother and I were facing. Our father, who was 86 and lived alone, was in the hospital, weak, depressed and no longer eating on a regular basis. He needed to be in a nursing home, but he was insisting on returning to his own house, determined to live independently. Any change for him, even if he agreed, would be a logistical challenge because my brother and I lived in different states, each about a twelve-hour drive from his home. To complicate matters, Dad refused to tell us anything about his finances.

"As easy as possible," I responded. Immediately Isaiah 22:22 came to mind: "I will place on his shoulder the key to the house of David; what he opens no one can shut, and what he shuts no one can open." I had heard an excellent teaching by Dutch Sheets, executive director of Christ For The Nations Institute, on that verse years before and had used it many times in prayer. This seemed to be an opportune time to apply it again.

"What doors do you want me to open?" I asked. I grabbed a scrap of paper and began to write down what came to mind. We needed to know his financial information in order to pay his bills. An assisted-living residence near his home would enable him to maintain contact with friends. Dad would have to agree to sell his home in order to pay expenses. We would also need a buyer for the house and its contents. It seemed a lot to ask.

With my list completed, I began my prayer: "Lord, I take the keys to the house of David, and I open the doors that need to be opened. I open the doors to accessing all of Dad's financial records, to placing him in the best living arrangements and to his agreeing to sell his house. I also open the door to the right buyer for the house. Whatever is opened with the keys cannot be shut. I lock the doors to the enemy's attempts to obstruct God's plans for my dad. Whatever I lock with these keys must remain locked. In Jesus' name, Amen."

Within two hours my brother called in total amazement. Not knowing that I had prayed that prayer, he reported, "It's incredible. Dad just gave me access to all his financial records. I can't believe it. Just like that!" I was as surprised as he was.

How did God do that? Dad had a reputation for stubbornness. Trying to convince him to change his mind about anything was about as easy as digging to China with a spoon.

With that hurdle out of the way, I thought the other details would fall into place with little or no effort. And they did for the most part. But God had more to teach me on this journey.

The next challenge was locating an assisted-living residence. Time was short. He would be discharged soon. My brother tried to get recommendations from the social worker, but she told him that hospital regulations restricted her from doing so. It was my turn to try. I called and explained the difficulty of evaluating dozens of homes long distance. Would she be willing to give me names of five reputable places that she personally would consider if placing one of her own family members? I copied down the names she offered. The key to the house of David had just opened another locked door. Then I enlisted my daughter's help.

"Amelia, we need to find out where God wants Grandpa to live. Will you listen with me?" We quieted ourselves and asked God if the right place was on our list of five. We both sensed that, yes, God was confirming in our hearts that it was. "Lord, would You show us which city it's in?" We waited. The same city came to both our minds. There were two homes in that location. "Lord, which home would be best for him?" We both felt directed to the same name and had great peace about it.

Only then did I look it up on the Internet. The website showed a beautiful Victorian home furnished with antiques. It looked more like a charming bed-and-breakfast inn than a nursing home—and it was just a few miles from his house. All the rooms were private. It sounded ideal except for one stipulation—he had to be continent. Dad had been using a catheter for the previous year or so. Had we not heard God correctly?

"Lord, what do I do now?" God directed me to call his urologist, who explained that my father had refused surgery to shrink his enlarged prostate gland, necessitating the catheter. Our only hope was to obtain his consent to a laser procedure. Dad, however, would not budge no matter what I said to convince him otherwise.

I sought God's advice again. This time John 3:8 popped into my thoughts: "The wind blows wherever it pleases. You hear its sound, but you cannot tell where it comes from or where it is going. So it is with everyone born of the Spirit." For two years God had repeatedly directed me to that verse, but I never understood what it meant—until I attended a conference featuring James Goll as the speaker. When he announced that verse as his topic, I wanted to shout, "At last!" With great relief I finally understood what God was saying, and it fit perfectly with this new predicament.

The analogy Goll used was that of a sailboat tacking into the wind. A boat that is tacking moves forward in a zigzag pattern: The sailor turns the bow so that the wind fills first one side of the sails and then the other, moving the boat forward. Likewise, instead of taking us from point A to point B in a straight line, the Holy Spirit often directs us on a zigzag course. We head one way until we can go no farther; then we are directed another way until we seem to land in a cul-de-sac, and so we tack back and forth until we reach the final destination. So it would be with transferring Dad to a nursing home.

God directed me to go ahead and schedule the laser procedure on a particular Friday. He impressed me not to call

Dad again until after that date. Tension mounted day after day as I wondered what would happen when the urologist showed up to do the procedure.

What a shock to hear that my father actually agreed to the laser surgery! We were home free, or so I thought. Days later, however, a nurse informed me of a complication following the procedure. I hung up the phone in frustration until I remembered my Isaiah 22:22 prayer. Faith rose within me. I declared emphatically, "My dad *will* go to that assisted-living home and nothing can stop it."

By the time we finally transferred Dad, God had provided a solution to every problem—the last being the sale of his home and its contents, which occurred quickly. The Holy Spirit walked us through every locked door. Or, to use the sailing analogy, we zigged and zagged all the way to the finish line. My father stayed at that home for three years, and every time I talked with him he thanked me for finding him such a wonderful place to live.

Just a word of caution about praying Isaiah 22:22. I do not pray this on a whim or to achieve selfish ends, but only when directed to do so by the Lord. If, for example, I were applying for a job that looked really appealing, I would not pray for God to open that door unless He directed me to. That job might appear awesome from my perspective, but only God knows the whole story. There might be hidden problems that only God can see.

Remember: The first step in any decision is to ascertain God's will. Only if God confirms His plan are we to use the key to the house of David to open any locked doors. Isaiah 22:22 is not a magic wand to wave whenever we are frustrated. Wisdom dictates we seek God's heart first to confirm His will. Then we can ask Him which doors to unlock and which ones to lock. Prayer is not about manipulating circumstances or people, but about following the Lord's specific guidance.

As you learn to apply these six secrets to power praying, you will begin to see the hand of God directing you in supernatural ways. This prepares you for the last secret.

Remember . . .

- God can make a way past any obstacle that blocks His plans for you.
- God will help you tack your way forward as the Holy Spirit directs your course.
- Not every open door is God's will for you. Pray for discernment.
- Is a locked door blocking the path that God has directed you to take? Use the key to the house of David to unlock it.

11

Secret #7:
Employ the Power
of Testimonies

It was Greg's last day with our family. He was heading back
to China for the summer, having spent the spring semester
of his junior year in high school living in our home. I was
going to take Greg to the airport, so we loaded up the car in
the predawn hours and headed out. About a mile from our
house I noticed the fuel gauge. I had less than a quarter of
a tank—not enough to reach the airport. How could I have
forgotten to fill the tank? We needed a gas station, but would
one be open at 4:30 a.m.? I explained the problem to Greg.

"God can fill the gas tank," he responded. His faith amazed
me. Greg had no spiritual framework before coming to the
United States as an international student, but he was curious about Christianity. Although he spent hours sequestered

in his room studying, the aroma of supper being prepared invariably enticed him into our kitchen to watch me cook. I gobbled up every opportunity to tell him "God stories"—testimonies—as I prepared meals. Now, after five months of hearing about supernatural answers to prayer, he had more faith in the miraculous than most believers. We did indeed find an open gas station, and our conversation the rest of the way to the terminal focused on Christ.

It is not necessary to be biblical superheroes in order to be change agents for Christ. Simply sharing what God is doing in our lives allows others to see how God uses ordinary people to do extraordinary things. The impossible becomes a reality when someone hears our testimonies. Then they begin to wonder, *Why not me?*

Learning to share testimonies came to me as another serendipity. As I conversed with friends, "God stories" would frequently come to the forefront of my mind. I did not realize God was speaking through these testimonies until a leader in my prayer group insisted that God wanted to use those experiences to teach others about Him. He challenged me to test it out.

From then on, if a "God story" came to mind when chatting with someone, I relayed it. Each time I got the same reaction. "That's amazing," the friend would say. "I really needed to hear that. Thanks for sharing it with me." As I realized the impact of these stories, I started praying, "God, if there is something You want me to say, have it come into my mind while I am talking. Block anything You don't want me to discuss."

The more I recounted my experiences with God, the more "God experiences" He gave me. The seeds I sowed into others began reaping a harvest of new supernatural occurrences in my own life.

Giving witness to what God is doing in your life causes a multiplication of similar occurrences. It increases your faith and the faith of those around you. The spiritual atmosphere changes because you are releasing God's truth and affecting the mindsets of those who hear. This creates the potential for your listeners to begin having supernatural experiences themselves.

Be prepared, however, for some interesting reactions. When I told a friend that I prayed about which dog pen to purchase for our new Maltese puppy, he raised his eyebrows, and his voice.

"You mean you actually *prayed* about what pen to buy? I never would have thought of that."

"Sure, why not?" I said. The one I liked was reasonably priced, but I read two negative reviews written by Maltese dog owners. Their comments made me question the wisdom of purchasing it. So I prayed, and as I waited I kept seeing an image of that pen. I asked for confirmation, and the image stayed in my mind along with peace about buying it. By following God's wisdom, not the reviews, we got a great pen for our dog.

Sharing that particular testimony might not cause my friend to pray about mundane decisions, but a seed has been planted to encourage him to think in more specific terms about depending on God for the wisdom he needs every day.

Sharing "God stories" might sound easy, but sometimes it comes with a cost. I was asked to give a devotional talk to a meeting of the board of trustees of our children's school, and I sensed that God was going to add something at the last minute. Sure enough, just minutes before the meeting began, tears came to my eyes as God reminded me of an unusual Christmas gift I had received years before. I did not relish the thought of being vulnerable by sharing the story. When it came time to speak, I presented my prepared material. As I finished the last few sentences the other story popped back into my mind. I knew God wanted me to give the following story.

A friend had given me a metal spike as a Christmas ornament. It represented one of the nails driven into Christ's body on the cross. At the time I thought, *What a gruesome gift! I don't want to put that on our tree.* But on Christmas Eve, after the family had gone to bed, I found the doll that my daughter had used to represent baby Jesus when she played Mary for a school Christmas pageant. I laid the baby at the base of our Christmas tree, wrapped in a purple blanket. Then I laid the nail on the baby's chest and wept as the enormity of Christ's sacrifice became real to me in that moment.

Tears flowed uncontrollably down my face as the board members sat listening in silence. My voice, barely audible, strained to finish the story and eke out a closing prayer. The meeting resumed as I sat dabbing an unbroken stream of tears, desperate to exit the room and find a private place to sob.

Giving your testimony may cost you tears, embarrassment, an invasion of your private moments with God and perhaps even criticism or ridicule. Ask Him to bring up the right story at the right time, and leave the results to Him. Pray for boldness to share. God enables those whose hearts are set on obedience.

Do I recount every story that pops into my mind? No, occasionally I start thinking about an experience but sense a check or hesitancy in my spirit. It could mean that the other person is not at a point in his or her spiritual journey to receive it. Or

I might be throwing godly pearls where they will be trampled upon or mocked. There are times, however, when I feel peace about sharing a story even though the other person has doubt or unbelief. Be judicious and let the Holy Spirit guide you.

Also, do not feel pressured to think up testimonies. They will come to you naturally as you yield your conversations to the Lord. If you have doubts about sharing, ask for confirmation. We must be mindful not to tell "God stories" in order to puff ourselves up or to convince someone that miracles are real. My spiritual mentor advised me: "God is pleased when we slow down at the yellow lights and stop at the red ones." God's timing and direction about when and what to share are vital. Trust His guidance.

When Amelia was a sophomore in college, God directed her through a dream to speak at a chapel service at her former high school. She dutifully prepared what she wanted to say. At nine o'clock the evening before, she asked if I would read her speech. Instead I asked, "Did you pray about what God wants you to say?" She left the room and returned shortly in extreme frustration.

"It's totally wrong. God showed me that I am supposed to give a personal testimony. I'll be up till midnight rewriting this." She retreated to her room to start over.

The next morning I sat in the darkened auditorium holding back tears as Amelia explained to the high schoolers how God used a dream to show her the wounds in her heart that needed His healing. She challenged the students to ask God to show them any hurts that needed His divine touch. "Knowing God in your head will not heal your heart," she explained. "Bring your hurts to Him and let Him heal them." The Lord's presence was powerful.

When I picked up Mark and Greg from school that afternoon they both exclaimed, "That was the best chapel we've had all year. Everyone was talking about it afterward." Her God-given testimony had touched many hearts.

God's fingerprints on my life became noticeable to me before I learned to hear Him speak. A Christian radio program in the 1980s challenged listeners to record their "God sightings" each day. Since every good gift comes from God (see James 1:17), I began to write down every blessing that I experienced. After several weeks of journaling, my spiritual antenna had been tuned to see God in the smallest occurrences.

I challenge you to start looking for God's handprint on your life and begin giving Him credit. Share your experiences with family members. Start with simple things like, "God gave me favor today. Someone let me go in front of her at the checkout line." Or "God blessed me this afternoon. A coworker treated me to lunch." Notice as you begin describing your "God stories" how He will multiply them. As you give Him credit for the simple things, He will start showing you the supernatural ones.

Just as Jesus demonstrated God's love and power, so we are to be living illustrations of the same to others. The Kingdom of God is within us. We reveal it by sharing our "God stories" with others. If we, like the servants whose master entrusted them with a number of talents, invest our spiritual experiences in others, more will be given to us (see Matthew 25:14–26). When we give praise and honor to God for what He is doing in our lives, we will see miracles multiply.

Luke 8:26–39 recounts Jesus' deliverance of a tormented man who lived among the tombs in the country of the Gerasenes. When the man was set free from a legion of demons,

Jesus told him, "Return home and tell how much God has done for you." Likewise we can spread the Good News and demonstrate a Christ-centered life by sharing our testimonies. Who knows? Your testimony might just pique the curiosity of your listeners to seek after God for themselves.

As you learn to apply the seven secrets to power praying, you will find that God is more than ready to guide and direct you. That is why the anticipation of hearing God excites me every time I sit down to pray. If the Creator of the universe wants to engage me and share His wisdom with me, I do not want to miss it.

We learned in part 1 to be in partnership with God, and we have learned in part 2 the seven secrets to power praying. As you practice the secrets, you will find that you are accessing God's wisdom with more ease and accuracy every day. Join me as we go even deeper into power praying for your needs and concerns—the ordinary and the seemingly impossible. This is the focus of part 3.

Remember . . .

- The more you repeat your "God stories," the more experiences He will give you.
- Your testimonies create the potential for your listeners to have their own "God stories."
- As you give Him credit for the simpler things, He will show you the supernatural ones.
- How did you see God today in your life? Share that with someone and see what happens.

Stepping Up *to* *the* Next Level

12

The Nuts and Bolts of Prayer

Have you ever tried to find something basic like a screwdriver in a toolbox? You sift through wrenches, hammers and drill bits; you pull out a level, a tape measure and a crowbar. At last, there on the bottom sits the tool you need. After numerous scavenger hunts through my husband's toolbox, I decided to have my own collection of screwdrivers in my dresser drawer.

Prayer can be like that. A crisis hits. Rather than go to God first for His remedy, we call a friend, hoping he or she has the right tools to fix whatever is wrong. Then we talk at length about the details of the crisis, all the while digging for that elusive tool.

This process, however, focuses on the problem, not the Solution. There will be times when we are uncertain how to pray and times when God directs us to pray with others, but as we learn to seek God first and apply the seven secrets to power praying we will acquire new tools for our own toolboxes. By focusing on the Lord first rather than going to a friend, we minimize the problem and magnify His power to overcome it.

In this part of the book, we will learn to hone our ability to ascertain His will accurately so that we can pray confidently. Let's get started!

Putting God First

Kick-start your power praying, as Jesus did, by drinking deeply of God's wisdom and presence first thing each morning. Just as patients fail to improve (or get worse) when they forget to take their medication, so we stagnate (or backslide) when we skip morning prayer time with God.

I can almost hear you saying: "But I've tried having devotions or reading the Bible in the morning. It just doesn't happen." Years ago I realized that my hectic lifestyle had compressed God into a convenient corner. I treated the Lord as an afterthought rather than a first thought. I solved all my problems through logic, reasoning or cash. Then I wondered why it was so difficult to read the Bible and obey His Word.

What was missing? I was more concerned about what my patients thought than what God thought. Several times in Scripture God tells us: "The fear of the LORD is the beginning of wisdom, and knowledge of the Holy One is understanding" (Proverbs 9:10; see also Job 28:28; Psalm 111:10). Without a worshipful fear or awe of God, I lacked wisdom. Instead of proactively preparing for each day I ended up stomping out wildfires.

One evening I implored the Lord to give me intense reverence for Him. I wanted conviction so deep that I could not live one day without His presence. His agenda and thoughts had to take precedence over mine. Determined not to quit praying no matter how long it took, I pleaded with God until, two hours later, a vivid image formed in my mind. It was of Moses' face when he met with God on Mount Sinai. He gripped the reddish, damp precipice and stared directly at me with eyes filled with awestruck wonder and trepidation as if to warn me, *Don't ever take God lightly again.*

Are you passionate about spending time with God? If not, now is the time to ask God for holy reverence for Him: "Lord, take away my self-reliance and my confidence in my flesh, and replace it with unshakable awe toward and dependence on You. Stir up hunger and thirst that drive me to seek Your presence every day." Pray it as though you mean it, and pray it until you receive it. This is serious business for you. No wimpy prayers here.

Please do not read any further until you determine whether or not God is your top priority. If not, why not? What has become more important than giving Him top ranking in your daily schedule?

Consecration

Before you throw off the covers, dig into your toolbox and pull out a power prayer of consecration that creates a spiritual mindset for the day. Mine consists of:

Offering my mind, will and emotions to God
Dedicating my time and talents to Him
Praying for protection for my family

The following is an example, not a formula:

125

Lord, I place my mind, will and emotions under the authority of the Holy Spirit. Guide and direct me today. I dedicate my time and talents to You. Help me use them wisely. Put a check in my spirit if I am making any unwise decisions, and help me mind the checks. Please put a hedge of protection around me and my family. Cover us with the blood of Jesus and release Your angels to protect us. In Jesus' name, Amen.

In the past my thoughts droned all day long like a beehive of discordant sounds—analyzing conversations, worrying about work, finances, family and what others were thinking. Moments of cerebral silence were rare. Now, after much practice, by consecrating myself completely to the Lord every morning, my mind is peaceful. God has free license to adjust my thoughts and emotions at any time. I try to keep one ear aimed "up," listening for His guidance even when I am in a meeting or engaged in conversation. Maintaining a peaceful mind helps me stay tuned to His frequency so that He can redirect me to wiser choices.

Preparation

Before heading off to work or diving into your to-do list, set aside time to prepare for your day. It helps to pair your daily quiet time with God with something habitual, or the rushing around to get ready will squeeze Him right out of the morning routine. Resolving not to brush your teeth or put on your shoes before honoring God first with time in prayer and the Word will cure any forgetfulness. As I mentioned earlier, I have determined that *No Bible, no breakfast.* My spiritual preparation for the day consists of several steps:

Thanking God for His blessings
Praising the Lord for who He is
Asking God, "What is on Your heart today?"
Asking what Scripture He wants me to read
Making Scripture-based declarations over my family

Thanksgiving and praise keep the Lord on the throne of our lives. They remind our heads and hearts that all provision flows from His grace. We are dependent upon Him for everything.

After asking God what is on His heart, follow by listening with a quiet mind. You will not hear anything if your thoughts are on the clock. Focus on Him. This morning when I listened to God's heart, He assured me that a difficult situation would work itself out over time and that I could relax and trust Him. That lifted a worry off my shoulders. At other times He might remind me of something He asked me to do that I have put off or direct me to a certain task. Listening to God's heart is when I often receive revelation about issues that are not on my immediate agenda.

If you do not sense anything, simply ask Him to guide and direct your steps that day. But listen again tomorrow. Do not pass up the opportunity for a supernatural heads-up on your day.

When you ask what Scripture to read, you give God the opportunity to speak to you personally through His Word. If you do not feel directed toward a specific chapter or verse, do not give up asking. You can default to Psalms, Proverbs, the Gospels or something from a devotional, but ask again tomorrow. Persistence pays off, and you will eventually be guided to specific readings. Whatever you read, ask the Holy

Spirit to open your mind to understand the words and their personal application. Record in your journal any verses that stand out.

One time the Lord directed me to Romans 8 three days in a row. Funny how numerous things went wrong during those three days! Each time I asked God what was going on, He redirected me to verse 28—that He is working all things for my good. Those three days trained me to focus on that truth and to stay peaceful when things jump out of joint. Does God direct me to a specific Scripture every day? No, but I never want to miss an opportunity to ask.

Finally, make declarations based on Scripture over your family, such as, "We are prospering and in good health, just as our souls prosper" (see 3 John 1:2; see appendix A for other examples). Once a year I ask God what He wants me to declare over myself and my family. I record them on index cards. I then declare them during my daily "God time." Again, if you do not sense anything yet from God, you can look up verses that pertain to blessing your family with good health, favor and provision. Scriptural prayers are powerful.

Having "God time" as you begin your day will have great impact on your relationship with the Lord. He is looking for those whose hearts are desperate for Him. Prayer time is not about reading so many verses and checking it off your to-do list. Pursue His presence passionately. It might seem awkward at first, but do it anyway. Praise Him and thank Him for what He has done in your life. Continue praising Him as you get dressed or drive to work. Engage your heart, not just your head.

The more your heart connects with the Lord each morning, the better equipped you will be to access His wisdom throughout the day. Just as you would not show up for work only two days a week and expect to get a paycheck for five, likewise, the spiritual payoff from prayer reflects the amount of time and passion you invest in it.

These are the basics of putting God first. Now let's explore where to start when you need help with a specific decision or a particular need.

When You Need an Answer

Setting physical and spiritual parameters enables you to hear more easily and accurately. Schedule extra time in the morning or later in the day in order to set up these parameters and to listen for His solutions.

Establish Physical Parameters

Find a quiet room where you can relax with no phones or distractions. Sitting outside can also tune you in to God's frequency and enable you to focus totally on Him. But beware: The enemy will try to throw you off track as you pursue God. The dog will start barking or the doorbell will ring more than usual. Ask God to block any interruption that is not essential and to protect your prayer time. Persevere. You are being tested, and you can pass the test. Do not give up.

Just as I do in my morning "God time," I enter His presence with thanksgiving and praise every time I come in prayer (see Psalm 100:4). This can be as simple as verbalizing thanks and praise. It can include listening to music, singing or taking a walk and admiring His creation. As we praise God from our hearts (not just our lips), His presence draws near (see Psalm 22:3).

Establish His Peace

Ask the Lord to quiet your mind and flesh, to take away distractions and to fill you with peace. It takes practice to tune out everything but Him. Feeling pressured or rushed is a warning to focus on the Lord, not on problems or time. If an offense surfaces, forgive the offender. If an idea persists in popping up, write it down in order to quiet your thoughts. Silencing the talking in your mind is absolutely essential for hearing God. Turn off the brain chatter.

Once my mind and flesh are quieted I pray:

Give me clarity of thought and the mind of Christ. Give me eyes to see You and ears to hear You. Please release a spirit of truth, wisdom, revelation, knowledge and wise counsel. Refill and refresh me with Your Spirit. Take authority over my thoughts.

Block Enemy Interference

Setting spiritual parameters for prayer is uncommon among some mainline denominations, which (for whatever reason) have failed to teach about spiritual warfare. Many believers are not aware that while God has a plan for their lives, the enemy does, too (see Ephesians 6:12). Scripture tells us that God disarmed the kingdom of darkness through Jesus' death on the cross, and that Christ gave us authority over all the power of the enemy (see Luke 10:19; Colossians 2:15). He expects us to exercise that authority. Satan would love to counterfeit God's voice and confuse us. Setting spiritual parameters to lock the enemy out of our prayers is essential.

First, turn James 4:7 into a declaration by stating out loud: "Lord, I submit myself to You. I resist the devil. He must flee, in Jesus' name." This affirms the Lord's sovereignty and establishes dominion over the enemy. Be confident the enemy has left. If you have any uncertainty about your authority, I recommend reading Dutch Sheets' book *Authority in Prayer* (see appendix C).

Second, use the keys to the Kingdom of heaven to bind or forbid on earth that which is forbidden in heaven and to loose or permit on earth that which is permitted in heaven (see Matthew 16:19). Lies, deception, demons and confusion do not exist in heaven. Jesus gave us the authority to forbid them from influencing us on earth.

Finally, ask the Lord to release angels to guard and protect you and your family and to cover you with the blood of Jesus for protection. We overcome the enemy by the blood of Christ and the word of our testimony (see Revelation 12:11). I include family in my prayers of protection, because I have found through experience that when I am engaged in spiritual matters, my family will sometimes experience harassment from the enemy.

Your prayer might sound something like this:

In Jesus' name I bind all the powers, communications, curses and assignments of the kingdom of darkness, and all lies, deceptions and confusion from manifesting against me and my family. Please cover us with the blood of Christ and release Your angels to protect us. Confuse the enemy and keep evil far from us.

Listening to God's Heart

Before posing any questions to the Lord, always honor Him first by asking what is on His heart. Even though you have already done this in the morning, listen for updates. Record whatever God says, highlighting it with a bullet point or a different colored ink so it stands out in your journal when you want to review exactly what the Lord said at some later date. If there is silence, that is fine. At least you have not missed the opportunity to hear what matters most to Him.

Seeking God's Wisdom

Are you ready to ask God for wisdom? This is the time to apply the first secret and any others that pertain to your situation. Your prayer might sound like this: "Lord, I need Your wisdom concerning (fill in the blank). I say yes to whatever You direct me to do. I give You permission to change my heart and mind to align with Yours."

Learning how to ask for wisdom is very important. When possible ask open-ended questions like, "What is Your truth about this?" and "What do You want me to do in this situation?"

When school let out one June, the kids wanted to know if we had a vacation planned that summer. My husband was between jobs so money was very tight; a vacation seemed impossible. But we asked God if there was something fun we could do.

Moravian Falls. His answer took me by surprise. I had expected to hear of museums and day excursions to places nearby, not a driving destination eight hours away. By posing an open-ended question, we heard God's heart for us and spent a wonderful two days there (see in chapter 19 how God funded that trip). Conversely, limiting the question to "What museums should we visit?" might have made it more difficult to ascertain God's agenda for us.

When it was my turn to prepare a devotional talk for a board meeting, I asked, "Lord, please show me what You want me to say." If I had asked, "Which do you want me to talk about, gratitude or stewardship?" the question might have been met with silence if neither was God's choice. If we pose either/or questions, we limit God to two choices, neither of which might be His desire for us.

If I am stuck in a mindset that needs to be changed, instead of giving me an answer, God will ask me a question. When Mark had an opportunity to attend a writer's conference some years ago, God asked, *Why wouldn't you let him go?* His question identified my fear that taking him out of school for several days might be frowned upon. My fear of man was interfering with God's plan. We received permission for him to miss school, thus eliminating my concern.

When I am praying with or for someone, God might direct me to ask a question to clarify the issue or to open my mind to other answers. Buying a snowboard pass for my son to use over his four-week winter break one year seemed like a no-brainer, yet I felt a hesitation in my spirit. When I asked God about it, instead of a yes or no answer, He told me to ask Mark if he planned to take a winter term class. That seemed odd since I already knew the answer, but I asked Mark anyway. Contrary to our last discussion, he had changed his mind. Weeks later he signed up for a class, leaving no time to snowboard that season.

When trying to decide which of several similar choices to purchase, I assign a number to each and add an additional number for "other" (in case I need to expand my search). Then I ask God to tell me which number is the best. If the Lord is silent, it might be because it is not the right timing, the right store or the right items. Then I broaden the question to "Lord, what is Your truth about this?"

Backdoor Answers

"May I come over for prayer?" My friend needed to make a major decision that would affect the next three years of her life, and she needed the answer by the next day. The gravity of sharing the responsibility for her choice unnerved me. What if we did not hear God correctly? We could not afford to make a mistake.

As we sat on my back porch listening for God's wisdom, the Lord told me to ask her about coloring hair. *Pardon me? I thought we were talking about something very important here. Hair color? What does that have to do with anything?* He repeated His directive over and over. I recognized that inner voice as the Lord's, but I was almost too embarrassed to repeat what He said. Fortunately, we were good enough friends that I could risk making a foolish mistake.

"I know this sounds strange, but God is telling me to ask you about hair color. Maybe we're so anxious we need to focus on something else until we can calm down."

My friend's explanation of the ins and outs of dying hair diverted our minds from the problem. We proceeded to pray about some of my concerns, planning to come back to her question at the end of our prayer, when the answer to her problem popped into my head. I looked up and smiled. "He wants you to go ahead with that plan." She had received a similar impression.

Anxiety and fear can act like filters that block our ability to hear God clearly. If a problem is so emotionally laden that we cannot access a peaceful state of mind, shifting our attention to something entirely neutral allows the Lord to drop the answer in while we are looking the other way, so to speak. Now when someone asks me to pray about a distressing situation, I leave it intentionally until the end of the prayer. Then out of the blue or through the backdoor comes God's answer while we are focused on something else.

The Sounds of Silence

The ratio of prayers to answers is not always 1:1. Many times we pray for wisdom and hear nothing. If this goes on for an extended period of time, it could be a signal from God to reevaluate. The following list is not exhaustive but might give you some idea why you are not hearing an answer from God:

- Your question might be restricting His answer. Rephrase it with something open-ended like "What do You want to show me about this?"
- It might not be the right time to be asking about the issue.
- Your motives might not be pure. Ask God to examine your heart.
- The problem might not be your responsibility.
- God might be testing your perseverance or faith by having you wait.
- You might not be ready to obey what He wants you to do.
- You might have set limits that restrict Him from giving you His best answer.

For a more complete discussion, check out *Forever Ruined for the Ordinary*. In it Joy Dawson gives an extensive list of reasons why answers to prayers are delayed.

Confirming What You Hear

Hearing God accurately is important; mistakes are not pleasant. What if I am not sure it is God speaking? If I have any doubt or lack peace, I ask for additional verification. Actually, I seek confirmation for most decisions, especially those that affect other people. I have three main ways of asking for confirmation:

"Lord, if this is from You, please repeat it."

"Lord, if I am hearing correctly, please confirm it another way."

"Lord, if I am perceiving accurately, please show me more details."

When praying with someone else, it is wise to pray silently for confirmation before you reveal what you think you have heard. This helps eliminate any wiggle room for the enemy to cause confusion. If he does not hear what you are trying to confirm, he cannot fake a confirmation.

If I hear, *Fly to the conference*, and ask for verification in a different format, I might see an image of a plane taking off or see myself at the airport, which confirms that I heard correctly. If I ask God to confirm it by showing me more details, I might hear the name of the airline or be directed to rent a car upon arriving.

What if you are praying with someone for wisdom and you both receive different answers? If the Lord confirms them both, then ask for more details. When my daughter was in the eighth grade, she needed a white graduation dress. Unable to find anything suitable, we sat in the department store and asked God where the dress was. I heard *bridal* and Amelia heard *children's*. It made no sense, and we did not know back then to ask for more details. We searched in the bridal section with no success. We trooped over to the children's section and found her dress on the rack of First Communion dresses. By putting the two words together, *children's bridal*, it made perfect sense.

As mentioned in a previous chapter, I do not ask God to confirm His directions through circumstances, although sometimes He throws one in as a bonus. I let God choose the type of confirmation so that I am not restricting Him.

My biggest struggle when I first tried listening prayer was discerning who was speaking—me or the Lord. Discerning His voice takes time and practice. Through trial and error I learned to recognize that God's voice is peaceful and loving. He does not use condemnation, pressure or guilt in communicating with us. He never contradicts the truth in Scripture.

If I am hearing myself, however, I might experience a sense of duty, obligation or "should," or I might feel anxious or fearful. A negative tone is a red flag. Seek confirmation and wise counsel when there is any doubt.

If the final choice is not clear, I make sure that I have prayed this: "Lord, You are not a God of confusion. I bind all lies, deceptions and confusion, and I loose Your Spirit of truth and wisdom to lead and guide me." Before proceeding I will continue to put the issue before the Lord until I have peace and confirmation.

In the next chapter, we will learn more about the enemy's attempts to deceive us and the authority God has given us over the enemy's power.

Remember . . .

- Talking at length about your troubles emphasizes the problem, not the Solution.
- Connecting your heart with God's in the morning better equips you to make godly decisions throughout your day.
- Setting spiritual parameters and obtaining confirmation are essential when asking for wisdom.
- Is anything more important than putting God first in your daily schedule?

13

Unmasking Deception

My need to find an apartment while attending medical school sent me searching through newspaper ads. One sounded quite appealing—sharing the upper level of a quaint two-story home with another female. Nothing seemed amiss as I walked through the charming apartment with high ceilings and spacious rooms. My future roommate was friendly and flexible—no conflicts there. Everything lined up: the price, the location and the layout.

Right before making a commitment, I sent up a quick prayer. *Lord, is there anything else that I need to know?* Without a second's thought, out popped this question: "I probably don't need to ask this, but you don't do drugs here, do you?"

Before I had a chance to beat myself up for asking such a stupid question, the young woman said, "Well, yes. My friends and I smoke marijuana on the weekends. Does that bother you?"

By God's grace I narrowly escaped a living arrangement that could have put me in legal jeopardy as well as endanger my future in medicine. What looked like a God-opened door was a snare. God does not want us unaware of the devil's schemes (see 2 Corinthians 2:11), but we need His help in uncovering them.

"Be alert and of sober mind. Your enemy the devil prowls around like a roaring lion looking for someone to devour" (1 Peter 5:8). Satan's enticements will be beautiful and appealing. That is why, even when something looks great, it is vital to confirm whether or not it is God's choice.

Romans 8:9 informs us that we are "living the life of the Spirit, *if the* [*Holy*] *Spirit* of God [really] dwells within you [*directs and controls* you]" (AMPLIFIED, emphasis added). Otherwise, we are living the life of the flesh. My flesh can make some poor decisions that seem smart at the time. The key to wise choices is determined by the measure to which we rely on God's Spirit. Listening to and following God's divine directives ensure we will be led by the Holy Spirit, not a spirit of deception. How do we know what His Spirit is saying? Ask, ask, ask and listen, listen, listen.

Does the Holy Spirit have full sway over your life? If you are not sure, ask the Lord to show you any areas where you are not fully surrendered to His Spirit. Why not do it right now?

Knowing Scripture safeguards us from Satan's lies. God's Word is the gold standard against which we judge our thoughts and actions, as well as things that pop into our heads at random moments.

"The heart is deceitful above all things, and desperately wicked; who can know it?" (Jeremiah 17:9 NKJV). If we cannot trust our own hearts, how do we know if we are deceived?

Unless we ask God to examine our hearts, we run the risk of being misled. David was wise enough to say, "Search me, O God, and know my heart! Try me and know my thoughts!" (Psalm 139:23 ESV).

King David's son Absalom might not have lost his life had he allowed God to search his heart. Ensnared by lust, greed and pride, he proclaimed himself king, usurping his father's rule, only to lose his life rather quickly. David was restored to the throne; his protection came from aligning his heart with God's. He did not manipulate the people or his circumstances, as Absalom did. David trusted that his God would work things out for his good, and He did.

We can avoid deception when we remain mindful of our human limitations and maintain our dependence on God's unlimited knowledge. Is lack of awareness, lack of training or pride keeping us from supernatural solutions to everyday problems? My prayer is that at the end of reading this book, every reader will be enthusiastic about sitting in God's presence and listening for His godly counsel.

Cloaking

"Mom, the computer's not working." I followed Mark back to the study to investigate the problem. Our high-tech equipment, however, did not respond to my low-tech solutions.

"Let's pray about it," I suggested.

"Mom, it's a *computer* problem." He exited the study with a frustrated look that told me I was being too spiritual. Before I could smooth my ruffled feathers and focus on prayer, he returned.

"It's cloaking," he said confidently. "You were right."

"Cloaking?" How could I be right about something I did not understand? Mark proceeded to remind me of the Star Trek term. The Romulan spaceship had a cloaking device rendering it invisible to the natural eye and enabling it to attack the *Enterprise* undetected. In other words, the enemy had put a kink in our computer, hoping we would not detect it. I took the cue.

"In the name of Jesus Christ, I break off any demonic assignments against this computer. I command it to be restored. You have no right to our possessions."

I simply exercised the authority that Jesus tells us we have in Luke 10:19: "Behold, I give you the authority to trample on serpents and scorpions, and over all the power of the enemy, and nothing shall by any means hurt you" (NKJV). The computer malfunction disappeared. Mark was back in business, and we had just discovered one of Satan's tricks.

When the LED readout on our almost new DVD player dropped the *o* in *hello*, I got really angry. I was not going to put up with it saying *hell* every time I wanted to watch a movie. I took authority over the kingdom of darkness and bound its powers (see Matthew 16:19). Hell has no right to be in our home. A number of authoritative commands later and the *o* reappeared.

I suspect the enemy loves fooling with electronics. After the cloaking lesson I started praying when an appliance or computer went on the blink, just to see if we really needed a repairman or if it required a spiritual fix. Our heat pump had given us a few headaches over the years. The next time a repairman diagnosed a malfunctioning valve, I decided to pray about it. When he returned with the new part a couple of weeks later, I received a surprising phone call.

"Ma'am, I decided to check your heat pump valve before installing the new one. I can't explain it, but the old valve is functioning perfectly. It makes no sense to me. But I can't in good conscience put in a new valve if you don't need one."

It made perfect sense to me. God had restored what the evil one had tried to destroy. That saved us hundreds of dollars.

Sometimes a computerized cash register malfunctions when it is my turn to check out. Silently binding the enemy and asking God to restore the equipment often produces results. Does it work every time? No, there are real equipment glitches that have nothing to do with spiritual warfare, but cloaking is more common than most would suspect. It never hurts to cover the bases.

Cloaking shows up frequently in the area of illness or infirmity. One day Mark and I ran errands off and on for three hours. When we returned home he complained of pain in one foot. I asked the usual Dr. Mom question: "Did you injure it?"

"No, Mom. We shopped for three hours. That's why it hurts."

Suspecting that something foul was afoot, I reached down, laid my hand on the affected area and commanded the pain to go away in Jesus' name. The discomfort left instantly.

Many illnesses and pains are not real. The enemy looks for opportunities to insert symptoms, hoping we will attribute them to a natural event rather than to cloaking. A few days ago my throat began to feel sore. I bound spirits of infirmity and affliction and commanded them to leave. Nothing changed, so I asked the Lord what was going on. He directed me to command lying signs and symptoms to leave. I did and the soreness left.

Perhaps one of the most frequent sources of deception is relying on our own knowledge as a substitute for God's wisdom. "Let no one deceive himself. If anyone among you seems to be wise in this age, let him become a fool that he may become wise. For the wisdom of this world is foolishness with God" (1 Corinthians 3:18–19 NKJV). If we humble ourselves and seek wise counsel the rewards are limitless.

Is it foolish to expect God to give us specific guidance when He promises to help us? His Word says: "Call to Me and *I will answer you and show you great and mighty things*, fenced in and hidden, *which you do not know* (do not distinguish and recognize, have knowledge of and understand)" (Jeremiah 33:3 AMPLIFIED, emphasis added). That verse is one of God's guarantees for any believer needing wisdom, yet many do not avail themselves of God's offer.

On one of our mission trips, I roomed with a young woman who complained of an upset stomach upon arrival in Brazil. She attributed it to something she ate. I bound any spirits of infirmity and affliction and commanded them to leave in Jesus' name. I can still see the surprise in her eyes when all the symptoms disappeared instantly. It is commonplace for us to assign our ailments to our circumstances. If we accept symptoms without praying, however, we may miss an opportunity for immediate relief without medication.

I am not suggesting that every ache and twitch is a spiritual assault from the dark side, but given reports that a high percentage of doctor's visits involves psychosomatic ailments, it does not hurt to bind any enemy assignments and pray for healing first. It just might cure the problem. By all means, however, it is important to see a physician if symptoms are urgent or persist.

Tricks of the Trade

Satan is the father of lies. As mentioned earlier, he wants to steal, kill and destroy God's children, but he does not advertise that fact. His lies are not often obvious; they are mixtures of truth and deception. He uses half-truths to prod and pressure us into making foolish decisions.

Just as he did with Eve in the Garden, Satan creates doubts about what God said. Did God really say they should not eat of *every* tree (see Genesis 3:1)? Just a twist of a word here and there and we start wondering what the truth is. He is especially adept at causing us to think that God is withholding good from us. Instead of being generous, we start clinging to and controlling our possessions because we believe the lie that provision is totally dependent on us.

Ananias sold land, lied about the selling price and withheld money promised to the apostles. Peter responded, "Ananias, how is it that Satan has so filled your heart that you have lied to the Holy Spirit and have kept for yourself some of the money you received for the land?" (Acts 5:3). Ananias did not trust God's provision. He wanted to control whatever he needed and deceived in order to do so.

What drives some to cheat on their taxes when Scripture tells us to pay our taxes? Or to keep extra change resulting from a cashier's mistake? If we doubt God's provision for all our needs, we may rationalize many ungodly decisions, but God sees our hearts. Do our choices honor the father of lies or the God of truth? God's wisdom lines up with the Word and draws us toward Christ. Deception leads us away from Christ and into ungodly behaviors.

One of the more common ways the enemy distracts us from God's plans is by throwing tempting activities our way.

We become sidetracked by filling our schedules without consulting God. Asking for and listening to the Lord's wisdom is more efficient than undoing poor choices made in haste.

Voice Recognition

If you are uncertain whether or not it is God speaking to you, pay attention to the feelings that accompany the communication. God draws us calmly toward wise choices, whereas the enemy pushes us to make snap decisions that we will regret later. God's voice is peaceful, loving and quiet; it flows into our minds like a gentle wave or a soft breeze. In contrast, the enemy's voice may be loud or harsh, associated with a sense of haste or coercion; or it may be quiet, but accompanied by fear, guilt or anxiety.

The spiritual battlefield is located between our ears. If you are not praying and a thought, picture or impression pops into your consciousness, do not assume it is from God. Ideas that replay in your mind may or may not be from Him either. While God often slips impressions into my thoughts, I do not presume they are all from Him. The enemy loves to deceive us with imitations. I confirm spontaneous impressions by silently asking God to erase any communications that are not of Him and to reiterate those that are in a different way.

If we meditate on the Word of God—if instead of just reading it we weave it into the fabric of our thinking—then our spirits will notify us when our thoughts, words or actions are in error or out of alignment with God. Avoiding deception requires being intentional and passionate about pleasing the Lord, discarding thoughts that oppose God's truth and conforming our minds to Christ's (see 2 Corinthians 10:5).

Do not underestimate the power of the Word as your defense against the enemy's lies.

Now that we are aware of the enemy's schemes, we can focus on God's interest in the practical details of our lives. Most of my "God stories" involve ordinary everyday occurrences that we all deal with, like the ones that follow.

Remember . . .

- Wise choices are determined by the measure to which you rely daily on God's Spirit.
- Be mindful of human limitations and maintain dependence on God's unlimited knowledge.
- Listening to the Lord's wisdom is more efficient than undoing poor choices made in haste.
- Are you daily weaving the Word of God into the fabric of your thinking as a protection against deception?

14

Day-to-Day Decisions

Making medical decisions was far easier than parenting and running a household full time. I could not write a prescription, hand it to my children and say, "See you in two weeks." I no longer had an assistant to take phone calls and clean up the room after me. When I lacked the answers in medicine, I had textbooks to turn to. My mother, who cared for the children in our home while I worked, soon moved into her own house. She had contributed to the smooth running of our family more than I realized. I was now on call 24/7 with no reprieve. Suddenly I felt bombarded by life.

What do we do when we must make choices that are not specifically addressed in Scripture? Seeking divine directions from God takes the guesswork and stress out of decision making. As mentioned in chapter 1, my first encounter with God's interest in the smallest details of everyday life involved finding a spot remover for the carpet. It has been an amazing sixteen-year journey. Following are some highlights that illustrate how to make decisions with a very personal God who wants to partner with us to do life—all of it. Answering the Reality Check questions at the end of each section will help you line up with God's heart.

Workplace Decisions

A friend who owns a plumbing business told me this amazing story. He was called to fix a leaky water pipe at someone's home. He and his assistant surveyed the long front yard, wondering where the break in the line was. It would cost the homeowner thousands of dollars if they dug up the entire water main. Would God show them where to dig? They each prayed briefly.

"Where do you think it is?" my friend asked his partner. The man pointed to a spot nearby. "That's where I think it is, too," my friend said. Indeed, they discovered the break at that exact location, saving the owner a bundle of money and sparing themselves wasted time and effort.

Toward the end of my private practice days, I was in the middle of biopsying an odd-looking rash that defied my clinical skills, when I heard the Lord speak the diagnosis into my spirit. I had not even asked Him! It had not been part of my differential, due to the unusual location, but the biopsy report verified the Lord's diagnosis. I wish I had known to ask the Lord about challenging diagnoses earlier in my career.

My daughter was working at a fast-food restaurant one morning and noticed her coworker suddenly acting strangely— wobbling on her feet, eyes fluttering. Was she on drugs? Just then the word *diabetic* flashed across Amelia's mind. She dismissed it, not having seen a diabetic person act that way.

Moments later the coworker collapsed. Amelia regretted not having acted on the impression and coming to her assistance. Fortunately, the woman was able to ask for juice to restore her blood sugar.

One of my friends inherited her father's metallurgy company. She runs it by seeking the Lord for His divine directions while learning as much as she can about a business for which she had no previous training. She presents most decisions to God and follows His directions with great success. She is an amazing example of being totally out of her comfort zone and totally dependent on the Lord.

God wants us to partner with Him to make wise choices no matter what our vocations. He has amazing solutions for every business decision you need to make. Have you thought about praying before meetings and asking God if there is anything He wants to show you? What about asking for His wisdom before signing contracts and negotiating deals? No problem is too big, too small or too complicated for God.

Reality Check

- Are my motives for asking pure—devoid of greed, envy, comparison and manipulation?
- Am I willing to lay down my agenda and listen with a neutral, submitted heart?
- Will I follow God's directions even if it means passing up a lucrative deal?

Stewardship

When financial lack pinched our pockets, God taught me generosity through the kindness of friends. As a physician,

I always expected to be on the giving end. It took time to work through the discomfort of being the recipient, but it opened my eyes to the importance of stewarding what God provides. As friends donated needed items to us, we donated clothes and household goods to others. Scripture instructs us: "Give, and [gifts] will be given to you. . . . For with the measure you deal out [with the measure you use when you confer benefits on others], it will be measured back to you" (Luke 6:38 AMPLIFIED). The more generous we became in giving, the more generosity boomeranged back at us.

Our upright freezer needed a new home. I wondered how much we could sell it for, but as I wiped down the shelves, the idea of donating the freezer to charity popped into my mind. I commented to my son, "I can't decide whether to sell it or donate it to charity."

"Follow your conscience," he replied.

In an instant my son's comment convicted me of focusing on money rather than stewardship. Why had I not asked God what to do? It should have been my first response, not my last. A few days later I watched with great pleasure as two men loaded it into a truck for charity.

That experience taught me to ask God if anyone in particular needs what we can no longer use. We had a desk in our study that was too large for the room. "Lord, who could use the desk?" The image of a friend popped into my mind. She was thrilled with my offer. While she was picking it up, I remembered a twin bed frame we had in the basement and asked if she could use that, too. Yes! Her daughter had just such a need. It is pure joy to follow God's lead and fulfill someone else's desires exactly.

Reality Check

- Am I seeking God's will in deciding how to steward His provision, or is my giving motivated solely by tax deductions or personal gain?
- Am I giving with a cheerful heart or out of duty or obligation?

Entertainment

As we have discussed, fiery darts from the enemy often come wrapped in enticing packages—particularly the enticement to sin. That is why God warns: "Among you there must not be even a hint of sexual immorality, or of any kind of impurity, or of greed, because these are improper for God's holy people" (Ephesians 5:3). The world of entertainment is a major source of enticement for improper behavior. Satan wants us to choose entertainment based on what the world is doing; God wants us to choose based on what the Word is saying.

As our children matured it was a challenge to determine which books, television shows and movies were appropriate. If prayer worked for shopping surely God would give us wisdom here, too. If I had doubts about a book, we prayed prior to purchasing it. If God did not give a yes or a no, I would ask Him to show me anything offensive as I flipped through the pages. At times this resulted in reshelving the book.

The day I overheard a popular TV cartoon promoting alternative lifestyles was the day I realized how dramatically television has changed since my youth. As I sat there in the pediatrician's waiting room, I wondered what messages children were absorbing from unmonitored television viewing. We opted instead for a select number of educational and family-friendly programs.

When purchasing what appeared to be family-friendly films, we sometimes relied on advertising blurbs instead of praying, only to find behavior that clashed with our Christian values. We talked about why it was not pleasing to the Lord and turned the movie off if it crossed our boundary of acceptability. A few ended up in the trash. The kids learned that values were more important than money.

For theater showings we based our decisions on Christian movie reviews like those offered in *Plugged In*. I could not shy away from 1 Corinthians 6:18: "Shun immorality and all sexual looseness [flee from impurity in thought, word, or deed]" (AMPLIFIED). When uncertain, I would ask myself, *Would I watch this movie with Jesus?*

Our choices as adults are equally as important in honoring the Lord as the ones we make for our children. I have often prayed, "Lord, cause those things that offend You to offend me." If we really think about Christ in us and with us, would our entertainment choices be different? Do we want the full measure of Christ to fill us or just the convenient measure?

Reality Check

- Am I choosing activities that honor the Lord and His Word, or am I going along with peer pressure, the latest trends or just plain curiosity?
- Am I willing to ask God what pleases Him and to choose something else if He says no?

Parenting

I wanted to be the perfect parent. Then we adopted our 21-month-old daughter. Amelia came with all sorts of blessings—like hyperactivity, developmental delays and a strong will. My type-A linear, analytic personality was no match for her high-spirited, capricious and determined-to-have-her-own-way temperament.

After a few frustrating years I came to the end of my parenting pride and threw myself on God's mercy. As I learned to depend on the Lord, I approached Him with problems—boatloads of them. I took 1 Peter 5:6–7 to heart: "Therefore, humble yourselves under the mighty hand of God . . . casting all your care upon Him, for He cares for you" (NKJV, emphasis added). Through all the ups and downs of family life, He faithfully provided answers that Tom and I never would have thought of—creative ones, simple ones, delightful ones.

During elementary school, Amelia was invited to a sleepover to celebrate a classmate's birthday. We did not know the family. I prayed and had no peace about letting her stay past nine o'clock. My decision collided with my daughter's wishes; it did not help matters that I could not give a specific reason. "I just don't have peace about it, and I have to be obedient" was all I could say to her protests.

At nine p.m. I sat waiting for Amelia in my car, bracing myself for her temper as I watched her silhouette approaching through the darkness. *Here it comes. Lord, help me.*

"Mom, thank you *so* much for picking me up," she said sweetly as she plopped into the passenger seat. I scrutinized her face. It looked like my daughter, but it sure did not sound like her! "They were about to show a scary movie with skeletons in it. I'm so glad I don't have to watch it." Unexpectedly

I had morphed from criminal to saint in my daughter's eyes. *Thank You, Lord.*

In contrast, years later when Amelia was invited to an overnight party by a high school classmate she did not know well, the Lord made it clear to let her go, even though my natural mind was unsettled about it. This would be a learning experience for both of us.

The next morning when I picked Amelia up there was a noticeable sigh of relief as she unfolded the events of the previous evening. After the host parents went to bed, the girls decided to watch an R-rated movie over her protests. With a pounding heart and sweaty palms, Amelia made a stand: "If you insist on watching this movie, then I'm going home." Despite continued criticism she held her ground. The girls eventually chose another movie. God allowed her faith and obedience to be tested and enabled her to resist peer pressure.

Following God's divine directives means approaching each request with an open mind and willingness to do whatever the Lord indicates. In the last example, my protective instincts would have said no to that sleepover. But God made it clear that she would be under His protection and that I needed to trust Him. We guard against creating a formula from one situation and applying it to a similar situation by seeking fresh guidance in every circumstance.

Reality Check

- Am I making decisions out of fear or pressure from my children, or am I seeking the Lord's directions and trusting His protection?
- Am I teaching my children to honor God's Word and to seek Him for godly choices?

Choosing a College

When it came time to choose colleges, we believed that God had a best choice for each child. Our job was to seek the Lord and follow His clues.

In the eighth grade, while attending an orchestra competition at a nearby university, Amelia had a strong impression that it was God's choice of college for her. The Lord confirmed this several more times over the next few years. It was the only school she applied to, yet she was denied admission. Despite subsequent applications and acceptances at four other colleges, she still believed her first choice was God's only choice for her. Two weeks after high school graduation she was accepted on appeal. It turned out to be a great choice for Amelia.

Mark's search looked entirely different. He was required to attend a college fair his freshman year in high school. Mark visited the booths and chatted with admissions reps right after proclaiming: "I don't even want to go to college." He emerged two hours later and announced excitedly, "I know what school I want to go to." Junior year he struggled with doubts about attending, but God confirmed to him that it was the best choice. He is currently a junior there.

Searching for God's college choice may seem daunting, but He has classmates, professors, courses and experiences waiting to be discovered. Begin by asking Him to bring to mind which schools to consider. If you already have a list, ask whether or not His pick is on that list. Ask God to highlight the right school and to cause the others to fade away in your mind. If you are touring colleges a simple prayer such as "Lord, show us Your will" suffices as you visit a campus or talk to a representative. Most importantly, follow up after each visit with "Lord, what is Your truth about this school?" Listen and see what He shows you.

When a friend asked me to join him in praying about three college possibilities for his daughter, one name came up in my mind repeatedly. I asked God to continue repeating it for confirmation or to erase it. The name continued to pop up in my mind, and my friend confirmed that it was the same name the Lord was giving him.

Parents would be wise to start praying for God's wisdom concerning their child's college choice well in advance of senior year. That way any directive that the Lord gives can be communicated before the child sets his or her heart on a particular location, size or type of school.

Pray for unity and peace in your family throughout the process. The key is listening for His directions. Leave the final decision to the Lord. Proceed when you receive confirmation and have peace that God is directing you.

Reality Check

- Do I believe that God's plan for my child's future is far better than I can dream or imagine, or must I control the outcome?
- Am I depending on God's guidance or letting a pros and cons list dictate which college my child attends?

Everyday Life

God has answers when we need to make decisions about our parents, children, vacations—even the weather. While visiting one of her relatives in Florida, a friend of mine was praying about an approaching hurricane. The Lord told her to walk around her relative's neighborhood and pray prayers of protection. She walked through the streets pleading the blood of Jesus over the homes. While they did experience heavy rain, none of the houses in the neighborhood was damaged, unlike those in the surrounding areas.

One evening my daughter had just left for a church program when the tornado sirens went off. I tuned into the weather report on television and saw that the area most at risk for a tornado was right over our church. I bound the enemy from causing a tornado to hit the church and asked the Lord to dissipate the strong winds. When Amelia returned home she told me that the pastor saw a funnel cloud heading right for the church, and then suddenly it lifted and passed over the area.

One Sunday night strong winds and heavy rain pummeled our region. We woke up to a leaking roof. Which roofer would be reliable, honest and quick to respond? As I sat and listened, I saw a picture of dog bones all over our roof and heard the name *Dry Bone Roofing*. Their estimator "happened" to arrive that afternoon at the same time as our insurance agent. Within an hour all the details of replacing our roof and having it covered by our homeowner's policy were wrapped up—a testimony to God's wisdom and efficiency.

I wrote earlier about my mother's accident. When it came time to transfer her from the hospital to a rehab facility, finding a top-notch nursing home was a very different challenge from finding one for my father.

I prayed numerous times but heard nothing. I looked at a few recommended places online but had no peace about them. One day as I was about to deposit a check at my mother's bank, the Lord directed me to ask the bank teller. When I mentioned our need, the teller's eyes lit up as she touted a

Christian facility five minutes from my mom's house. She received outstanding medical care and physical therapy there before being discharged back home two months later. God had provided a stress-free solution.

Power praying is a wonderful asset while driving. If traffic comes to a standstill, I ask the Lord whether to stay put, switch lanes or exit. It is amazing to find out that He has directed me to a certain lane to avoid an accident or that I am in the correct lane for merging. When I first tried this, any anxiety or fear about traffic or road conditions caused me to hear my fear speaking rather than the Lord. Those mistakes, however, taught me to recognize His gentle, peaceful voice, thus saving time and frustration in the future.

On one vacation Mark and I left the family on the beach and drove back to the condo for something. Upon our return the parking lot looked full. We needed a space in the first row so that my mother would not have to walk any distance to the car. I headed for the front of the lot. A quick glance confirmed there were no spaces. But that was not quite accurate.

"Mom, angels drive blue Volvos." My son comes up with some witty remarks, but that one took me by surprise. He pointed to an empty spot a few cars away. How had I missed it? Mark told me that he saw a blue Volvo in the space, then watched it back partway out and disappear into thin air. God was holding that spot for my mom, all because Mark had asked God for a close parking space.

God's ways are higher and better than ours (see Isaiah 55:9). I became a full-time mom when Mark was three years old. Conventional wisdom says to enroll children in preschool at that age, but I wanted to enjoy each day with my son. Would he suffer some horrible academic setback if I kept him home and bucked the world's wisdom? I am grateful that the Lord directed me to keep him home, not just that year but the next year as well. He knew the best plan for both of us, and I cherish those memories.

Have you ever prayed for a lost object? Sometimes the Lord tells me where to look. Many times I have no sense of where the lost item is but find other important things in the process of searching. I love my friend's story. Her daughter left her orthodontic retainer on a cafeteria tray at school. When she came home without it, my friend rushed to the school. She located a janitor, explained the problem and asked for permission to look through the garbage. The janitor escorted her to the Dumpster area, where numerous black garbage bags sat waiting for pickup. How could they possibly find the lost retainer? She and the janitor prayed that God would show them the right bag. They pointed to the same one, opened it and there sat the retainer right on top!

Reality Check

- Am I open to unusual directions from God, or do His plans have to make sense before I obey?
- Do I need to understand how everything will fit together before I say yes to Him?
- Am I following God's divine directions, or conventional wisdom?

Medical Decisions

Whenever symptoms of an illness occur, instead of relying solely on my medical training, my default is to ask God what the source of the malady is. My first question is always, "Is

this real disease or cloaking?" If it is real, I f
questions like, "Is the sore throat strep or just a
I ask about headaches, God often reveals a sour
or stress, thus enabling us to deal with the caus
nating the need for medication.

I have nothing against doctors or medicine; after all, God called me into the medical field as He did many others. In honoring God first as our heavenly physician, however, I find that symptoms are often resolved with prayer. If not, I ask for His wisdom and follow His directives regarding medical follow-through.

Scripture gives us four examples of Jesus healing five blind men—through touch, spit and clay, the spoken word, and spit alone. Notice there is no formula for healing the same condition. Likewise, we need to seek the Lord's divine directives on how He wants to heal in each instance. We are to be led by God's Spirit, not by our flesh or formulas.

Lately I have been troubled with indigestion. When I prayed about the cause I heard the word *neutralization* and saw *pH* printed in my mind's eye. Those two words indicated to me that my stomach was too acidic. The Lord directed me to eat certain alkalinizing foods. That led me to the Internet to verify if I had heard correctly. Sure enough, natural remedies for decreasing stomach acid include those items.

During one time of unemployment, we had to decide whether or not to purchase COBRA health insurance to tide us over until Tom's next job. When I prayed I saw the head of a cobra snake cut off. Tom agreed that we did not need to buy interim insurance this time even though we had done so in the past. God protected our health, and His wisdom saved us thousands of dollars.

If I do not hear anything from God and the matter is urgent, I check with a medical professional right away. If the Lord is silent and it is not urgent, I follow traditional medical practice, meaning I will take a decongestant for a cold or pain relief medication for a muscle ache, and continue to pray for healing.

Any time symptoms persist, it is wise to seek professional medical care.

Reality Check

- Assuming the medical need is not an emergency and the symptoms are not persistent, how do I make decisions about medical care? Are my actions driven by fear or worry, or am I willing to take the time to pray and ascertain the source of the symptoms and how God wants to treat the problem?
- Am I automatically running to the medicine cabinet before praying for healing and asking for God's wisdom?

Employment

God places believers in all fields of employment. If you are unemployed, He has a specific job for you. To find your match, engage God throughout your search. Commit the entire process to Him. Ask Him to connect you with the right contacts and support groups. Each day ask, "What is the next step, Lord?" Then listen for His guidance. Keep checking back and follow His directions.

We do not always sense His presence or receive specific directions with every prayer, but when our hearts declare, "I want Your best; I will follow You wherever that leads,"

He opens doors of opportunity. One of my favorite verses is Proverbs 16:3: "Roll your works upon the Lord [commit and trust them wholly to Him; He will cause your thoughts to become agreeable to His will, and] so shall your plans be established and succeed" (AMPLIFIED). You might not even be aware that He is conforming your thoughts to His as you daily seek His will and listen, but you will see incredible results when you do.

My friend received confirmation about taking a part-time job, not knowing it was only for a season. A few years later, the Lord directed her to quit and stay home. We may like the comfort of the familiar, but we need to be sensitive to the changes God wants to implement in our lives. Conflict in the workplace does not automatically mean it is time to leave. Ask the Lord if He is indicating a move or a change of some sort.

Whether you are hoping to switch careers or change jobs, God has an ideal place to position you for maximum blessings. Remember, though, that what appears to be a fantastic offer could have hidden snares. God is all-knowing; He sees what we cannot see. Ask for His wisdom when contemplating a new job or career change. If you have more than one offer, ask God to highlight the best one and cause the other offers to fade away in your mind. Always seek confirmation when making major decisions.

If you are married with children, have you asked if it is the Lord's will for both parents to work versus one staying at home? Are you working merely to raise your standard of living or because the Lord has called you to that job? God confirmed my employment as a dermatologist, but He also confirmed my leaving that position. Is the Lord the One who is determining your provision and your career?

Reality Check

- Am I assuming that every open door and every opportunity is from God, or am I willing to pass it up if God says no?
- Am I motivated by salary and lifestyle or by God's will for my life?

Who Is Your Author?

Christ is the Author of our salvation, but He is also the Author of our todays and our tomorrows. Do you want to be the sole manager of your life and miss His finest plan, or do you want Him to direct your decisions? If you are single, is God choosing your mate, or are you? If you are unemployed, is the Lord directing your search, or are you doing it on your own? If you own a business, who is calling the shots? Who is writing the story of *your* life?

Are you weary of striving to know God's will? Prayer does not need to be complicated: "Show me Your choice, Lord" and "Confirm if this is Your will" are simple prayers to pray. They are effective when we continue to seek God daily, to spend time in His Word and to listen for His answers.

I can almost hear you say this: "Getting answers for day-to-day needs makes sense, but I need a miracle—and I've never seen a miracle in answer to prayer."

Then let me ask, Would you like that to change? If it is possible for me, it is certainly possible for you. Read on and you will see what I mean.

Remember . . .

- Divine directions from God take the guesswork and stress out of decision making.
- Satan wants us to make choices based on what the world is doing; God wants us to choose based on what His Word is saying.
- We avoid formulas by seeking fresh guidance in every situation.
- Are you willing to look to God for every need?

15

Praying for the Impossible

The thief forced his entry through a side door and burglarized the home of my best friend. The next evening our Bible study group gathered to pray for her. The requests, including mine, centered on comfort and peace—the usual prayer fare. Then, surprisingly, one friend prayed that the thief would be caught and the valuables returned. I remember my embarrassment. *How naïve to pray that the stolen items would be recovered! Those things are in a pawn shop by now. What was she thinking?*

Instead of being humbled by my unbelief, I discredited her childlike confidence. After all, my generic prayers posed no risk to my reputation. Why be foolish?

Thus, I was stunned to hear a few days later that the thief had been caught and all the valuables returned. What if my friend had not prayed in faith? It was a watershed moment for me and the beginning of surprising answers to impossible prayers.

Years later, one spring day when Mark and Amelia were small, we were enjoying an imaginary picnic on the family room carpet. Lying on our picnic blanket, my head propped on my right hand, I pretended to eat the plastic hamburger and cookies. Thirty minutes later I stood up and buckled over in excruciating pain. The pressure from leaning on my right arm had torn my rotator cuff. I could not raise my arm more than waist high. The torn tendons would probably require surgery, but I wondered if God would heal me. Was there any harm in asking?

"Lord, *please* help me. You are my heavenly physician. Should I call a doctor, or will You heal my arm?"

As I waited on the Lord, peace replaced my panic. I heard a quiet, inner voice in my spirit telling me that God would repair the damage. I rejoiced at His promise, relieved to avoid surgery. Yet day after day nothing changed, despite continued prayer. Over-the-counter anti-inflammatory medication produced only minimal, temporary relief. I still could not raise my arm without agonizing pain.

As months passed, I began to question myself and God. I had no prejudice against doctors or surgery. Up to that point in my life, I had always defaulted instinctively to traditional medicine as the solution to any healing need. Stepping into the realm of spiritual guidance for a medical problem was unnatural and uncomfortable. Was I being foolish to expect God to heal my arm? Had I heard correctly? I had to be certain. So I asked again and again. My queries were met with either silence or another confirmation of His promise to heal, even though the severity of the pain and the limited range of mobility had not changed one iota since the injury in April.

More months passed. What was taking so long? Had God changed His mind? Prayer with a more mature believer brought the same assurance of healing. It made no sense to keep waiting, yet I felt constrained in my spirit to do so.

One Friday morning in October I awoke at 5:30 a.m. Anger consumed my thoughts. The knife-like pain had exhausted my patience. In anguish I cried out to the Lord: "God, I am *really* angry. I can't keep on like this. If I'm deceived, *please* tell me. This is the last time I will ask. If You're not going to heal me, I'll make an appointment with a surgeon on Monday."

His response shocked me: *You are healed; now start thanking Me for it.*

The firm tone with which those words were spoken into my thoughts brought conviction but not condemnation. At last. I knew that I knew that God had spoken to me. To my mind it made no sense to thank Him without any evidence of healing, but, from then on, even though the pain continued unabated, I voiced my gratitude each day to the Lord.

Two weeks later, during bedtime prayers with my daughter, I heard the quiet inner voice of the Lord: *Tomorrow your arm will be healed.* My reaction was a mixture of wonder and excitement. *Dare I believe this after seven months?* The next morning I awoke and raised my arm above my shoulder, pain-free! I swung my arm in circles and picked up something heavy. What had been impossible was now effortless.

The same Sunday morning that my arm was healed, a woman who had been paralyzed from the neck down in a skiing accident testified in church that God had completely restored her mobility. I had never heard of anyone being healed of paralysis. What an extraordinary morning! Had God coordinated my healing to coincide with her testimony as a double confirmation that He is still in the miracle-making business? It was too amazing to be a coincidence.

There were more challenges ahead that would stretch the limits of my reasoning, but they would also increase my passion and hunger to pray for the impossible. One of them occurred on a youth mission trip to Curitiba, Brazil, with a mission organization called Global Awakening.

I had volunteered to be a team leader. My team was ministering alongside interpreters in a simple, concrete-walled church. After the sermon anyone who needed healing was invited to come up to one of our team members for prayer. A middle-aged woman grabbed my arm and led me to her elderly mother. Through the interpreter I learned that fifteen years earlier the woman's mother had been in a severe auto accident in which her father had been killed. Her mother was left with a shattered leg that had to be screwed together. Ever since the accident she had limped around with a cane, in constant pain. The daughter asked if I would pray for God to heal her mother's leg.

I easily pictured in my mind the metal screws that were lining her femur. Although it was medically impossible to change her physical state, I remembered that Randy Clark, head of Global Awakening, had experienced miraculous answers to prayer for those with metal in their bodies. I had even seen a video of a man with a metal rod down his spine who, after prayer, was able to bend his torso backward and forward, pain-free, which was not physically possible from a medical standpoint.

Now here I was with a woman whose time-worn face looked at me with only the smallest glimmer of hope. Her daughter, however, brimmed with expectancy. How could I not pray? My faith was smaller than a mustard seed, if I had any at all. What I really wanted to do was pray for myself to disappear, but I dutifully laid my hands on her left leg and asked God to take away all the pain. Within minutes she admitted to some relief, so I pressed in for more. After about fifteen minutes she stood up with no pain! Only God knows who was more surprised—her or me!

But that was not the end. I moved on to pray for someone else. After I finished that prayer, the daughter came back to me with an interpreter and pulled me once again toward her mother. They had forgotten to tell me that the surgery on her mother's left leg had rendered it shorter than the other. Would I pray for God to lengthen her leg?

Oh, goodness! The first prayer had been risky enough for one night; the second request would really require going out on a spiritual limb. The concrete floor did not appear to have an escape hatch, so I sat across from the mother and had her extend both legs out in front of her. As I held the heels of her shoes it was obvious that indeed the left leg was about an inch and a half shorter than the right one. Would God be willing to perform two miracles for the same person on the same night? Through an ordinary person like me?

The risk level had increased a hundredfold in my mind, but that did not seem to bother God. I had to make a decision. Would I step out in faith or turn away? Intellectually I knew that my job was simply to pray and leave the results to God, but emotionally I battled with how I would feel if nothing happened.

I attempted a smile as I held both feet and began to pray. At least she would feel loved if I prayed, even if nothing changed. At first it was difficult to ascertain if any growth was occurring. I turned my head away while praying, hoping that there would be a noticeable difference when I looked at her feet again. During what seemed like an hour, but was probably only thirty minutes, an almost imperceptible lengthening of her leg occurred until both soles of her shoes were parallel. Did we ever rejoice! Her healing gave new meaning to the Scripture, "With man this is impossible, but with God all things are possible" (Matthew 19:26). A sliver of faith mixed with obedience opened the door to the miraculous, something traditional medicine could not have done for this woman.

The Old and New Testaments are filled with ordinary people experiencing extraordinary manifestations of God's power. Sarah bore Isaac at the age of ninety years (see Genesis 17:17). Gideon and his three hundred men routed tens of thousands of Midianite soldiers by blowing trumpets and breaking jars (see Judges 7:20–21). When Joshua and his army fought the Amorites, he commanded the sun to stand still, and God rained down hailstones large enough to kill their enemies (see Joshua 10:11–13).

Well-known biblical figures often lived average lives before they experienced their miracles. Sarah was a housewife; Joshua was Moses' assistant; and Gideon, a farmer, described himself as "the least in my family" (Judges 6:15). Ordinary résumés qualify us, too.

In the New Testament, Philip was told by an angel to go south along the road in the desert that headed toward Gaza from Jerusalem. Once there he was told by the Holy Spirit to introduce himself to an Ethiopian man traveling in a chariot.

After leading this man to faith in Christ and baptizing him, Philip was instantly transported by the Holy Spirit from that desert road to a town called Azotus (see Acts 8:26–40).

Paul's handkerchiefs were laid on the sick and the people were healed (see Acts 19:12). Paul had persecuted Christians before becoming a believer—proof that even the worst of sinners can be used by God to display His miraculous power.

In Luke 10:1–9, Jesus sent 72 believers out to the neighboring cities to heal the sick. This is consistent with Mark 16:17–18, where Jesus stated that miraculous signs will follow those who believe. He did not qualify "those who believe" by limiting His commission to the twelve disciples, to clergy or to any subcategory of believers. He included all believers, title or no title.

When we pray in the face of insurmountable odds, God does not consult statistics, write our request in the "impossible" column and move on to the next prayer. Whether we are trying to find a job when unemployment rates are high or sell a home during a housing recession, God wants us to live in the confidence of who He is. Is anything too difficult for the Creator of the universe? He delights in our impossible requests, large or small.

Praying impossible prayers means we may have to swallow our pride, look foolish in front of family or friends and risk having our petitions appear to go unanswered. It is the price we pay to see God's extraordinary responses. His divine interventions assure us that He alone receives the praise and glory. Like Joshua, we might have to walk around Jericho a few times to experience a miracle, but God's grace will enable us to wait on His answer even through periods of doubt and uncertainty. We do not need to understand completely in order to obey God. Believing God for supernatural answers is not always easy, but when we desire His will above all else, the rewards far outweigh the costs.

What is your need today? Is it money to pay bills, healing in your body or a restored relationship? Go ahead and ask. Tell Him what is on your heart. Believe Him for the impossible. Is anything too hard for God?

Remember . . .

- A sliver of faith plus obedience produces the miraculous.
- The least of us can be used by God for miracles.
- Pray in the confidence of who God is, not who you are.
- Is anything you are facing too difficult for the Creator of the universe?

16

Accessing God's Provision

Two boats sat by the Sea of Galilee. Jesus stepped into one and asked the owner, Simon, to put out into the water in order to teach the large crowd that had gathered to hear Him. Afterward He directed Simon to launch out into deeper water and let down his nets for a catch.

"Master, we have toiled all night and caught nothing; nevertheless at *Your word* I will let down the net" (Luke 5:5 NKJV, emphasis added). The authority in Christ's teaching minutes before must have resonated in Simon's spirit. His reward for obeying a divine directive that did not make sense resulted in a haul of fish that filled not just one boat but two.

Imagine a carpenter telling you how to run your bank, your business or your medical practice. Simon knew from personal experience there were no fish to catch. Yet by obeying the Lord's divine directions, he received a double portion. All the more reason to learn to listen to God.

What boat are you trusting to bring in your provision? Mine was dermatology. It supplied more than our necessities. My need for a personal relationship with God was more important—but I did not know that at the time. I captained my ship my way. Although I prayed for wisdom, God did not figure into my decisions. And, as I mentioned, I thought I was a pretty good Christian. You know—church on Sunday, tithing, charitable giving—the basics.

God had ideas I was not prepared for. I hung up my white coat and wondered if I had hung up my future and all my dreams as well.

When money is no object, it is easy to make decisions without the Lord's input. Giving up my salary with Tom also out of work forced a dependency upon God for wisdom. Our financial straits provided the ideal learning lab for spiritual growth and maturity.

God's teaching about provision started with a penny. I never expected my first trip to the grocery store as a newly unemployed stay-at-home mom to be my first experience with supernatural provision. The possibility of losing everything in a lawsuit stoked the fires of financial insecurity in my mind. I cautiously put items into our cart, careful to avoid spontaneous purchases. At the checkout a young cashier handed me a penny.

"What's this for?" I asked in bewilderment.

"Wouldn't your son like to ride the purple dinosaur?"

That penny, like manna from heaven, overwhelmed me with God's grace. I imagined God looking at me and saying, "Don't ever doubt My ability to supply. Don't ever question My goodness." If God cared about pennies, surely He would provide for all of our needs. The Lord had demonstrated to me His attention to the tiniest details of our family's needs.

Next, God signed me up for a class in humility. A friend introduced me to a new experience: shopping at a thrift store. Although I was an expert penny pincher, raised by a frugal Scottish-American mother who taught us the value of a dollar, the thrift store was an eye opener even for a bargain hunter like me.

I slipped down aisles of worn, donated clothing, past shoppers wearing thread-bare, stained garments, conscious of my clean winter jacket and wondering, *What am I doing here?* Would this be the story of the rest of my life? It turned out to be the first of many visits.

God taught me the value of praying for treasures amongst those jammed racks of hand-me-downs. My children and I began to thrill over our bargain-hunting prowess as we carted home a plastic bag full of riches for five or ten dollars. The Lord is our supply in seasons of plenty and seasons of lack. That season taught us to be conscious of His provision and our dependency on Him.

God taught me how to stretch a dollar further than I could imagine, but He also let me see that He delights to give good gifts to His children. Who would have thought my son's desire for a black leather coat and a tuxedo could be met at a thrift store at bargain prices? When my daughter wanted capris, I suggested she pray. Within seconds she found a twenty-dollar bill folded up into a one-inch square lying at her feet. That is the power of prayer.

The Lord kept the Israelites' clothing and sandals from wearing out for the forty years they wandered in the desert (see Deuteronomy 29:5). Part of God's provision for our family has been to extend the life of our cars and appliances. Four years ago I had lunch with Brook, a young adult I met on a mission trip. Afterward we sat in my car to pray before saying good-bye. "God wants us to pray for your car," she said. We both sensed that God wanted to extend its life until I could afford to replace it.

My current car is now fourteen years old with more than a quarter of a million miles on it. My husband's last car was sixteen years old before it died. The average lifespan of a refrigerator and a water heater is fourteen years, and a stove, sixteen years. By God's grace ours are all 25 years old or older. If finances are tight, have you considered praying that God would extend the life of your possessions?

God is still in the multiplication business. Once, I put four one-dollar bills into my pocket, but at the checkout I pulled out a ten, a five and two ones. On another occasion I pulled up to the gas pump with only a quarter of a tank left. The pump shut off at just over five dollars. Not wishing to pull up to another pump to finish refueling, I started the engine to drive off. The fuel gauge registered full! It should have cost more than thirty dollars.

During a mission trip we used six lunches to feed forty people. Food multiplied in front of us just as it did in the New Testament.

These experiences do not happen every day, but praying for multiplication is a routine part of my weekly prayers. There are so many ministries that need funding. How great would it be if believers prayed for multiplication in order to finance God's Kingdom on earth!

Meet my friends Jerry and Tracy Reiner, founders of the Project 5 2 (five two) ministry. Jerry worked in the merger and acquisition business until eight years ago. The Christian firm he worked for gave him Thursdays off to follow his passion—delivering leftover bread from a bakery to the needy. After two years God turned up the heat and Jerry began to feel unsettled. His wrestling with God took the form of questions like, "God, who's taking care of the single moms in the city? Who's taking food baskets come the first of January?" Churches fed the hungry during Thanksgiving and Christmas, but what about the other months?

God's response challenged Jerry: *What are you going to do about it? You've assessed really well what My Church is lacking, but what are you personally going to do as a family about these issues?*

"So I took a step of faith," he says. "I left the business and said to Tracy, 'This is going to sound wild, but I am going to leave this industry. Either I didn't hear from God and we lose our house in ninety days, or I did hear and God will provide for us. We are either going to stand on the Word of God or we're not.'"

Within two weeks a friend called Jerry out of the blue, wanting to catch up over lunch. Jerry shared his vision to provide for the poor and spread the Gospel.

"I want to pick up your mortgage starting this month," his friend offered.

God's confirmation that they were on the right track could not have been clearer. The ministry snowballed immediately. Jerry would deliver some of the donated leftover bread to a food pantry. If they had extra canned goods he picked them up and donated those to his next drop-off spots, wherever there was a need. He took any surplus from those centers and distributed it to the next centers on his drop-off route. When he outgrew his truck, someone donated a fifteen-passenger van.

What began with picking up bread from one store has now mushroomed into donations from 23 local restaurants. In the last six weeks he has received twelve tractor-trailer loads of food. His network of fifteen ministries has grown to about two hundred ministries who understand what Acts 2 and 4 are all about. Some churches have invested in trucks and warehouses to help with the distribution. His core churches are black, white, Hispanic, Protestant, Catholic—a blend that cuts across cultural and denominational lines.

Five years ago Jerry was invited to minister in the Appalachian Mountains in eastern Kentucky. For the first eight or nine months they simply delivered food and clothing wrapped in love, focusing on building relationships before they shared the Gospel.

Tracy told me about one young woman who woke up on Thanksgiving Day with empty cupboards—not a can of food to feed her two mentally disabled siblings or herself. Members of Jerry's network arrived with a box filled with turkey, green beans, sweet potatoes and all the trimmings. The woman commented to Tracy, "When they left, I could *feel* something different. There was something in our trailer that wasn't there before." Since then not only has she received Christ as her Savior, but so has her entire family. Every day she witnesses to people in her community about what Jesus has done for her.

"It's sparked me to pray for a hundred more just like her," says Jerry. His vision is to see twenty more distribution hubs along the Appalachian Trail from Georgia to Maine. "I believe God is going to connect the dots as I start pioneering and setting up other cities. Churches will follow. That's the vision. It's the Gospel 101."

On one occasion they took six students from a local Christian high school down to Kentucky to go door to door ministering to people. One woman wanted prayer for her knee. She was scheduled to have surgery two days later. The six young girls laid hands on the woman's knee and asked God to heal her. That Friday she visited her doctor. He reexamined her knee, declared that it was perfect and canceled the surgery. Through Project 5 2 God is supplying not only food and clothing, but supernatural healing as well.

Tracy occasionally works part-time as a dental hygienist, but more than 90 percent of what they need is met through prayer. I asked Tracy what were the hardest times living by faith.

"The early days were tough—birthdays, wanting to go on a vacation and not having the money. I told the Lord, 'We're going to give You our lives. We're Yours to do with what You want, but the bills are also Yours from this point on.'" Depending on the Lord for everything and seeking the Lord for every decision has been difficult, at times, as a family. Sometimes they could not meet payments on time, but the Lord always caught them up later. It is amazing to see that they have two children in a private Christian high school and one attending a private Christian university. Is anything too hard for God?

I share the Reiners' story to build your faith in an amazing God who promises to supply "all your needs according to the riches of his glory in Christ Jesus" (Philippians 4:19). The Reiner family takes God at His word. As they depend on God to provide, they see that "no matter how many promises God has made, they are 'Yes' in Christ" (2 Corinthians 1:20).

Not everyone is called to quit his or her job and live by faith. God needs Christians in the marketplace, the entertainment industry, the media and every facet of our culture. But wherever He calls us, He promises to supply.

God blesses us and others through us when we include Him in all our decisions. In the Old Testament God's people were instructed to tithe (give a tenth of their income) to the Lord, and in turn God promised to open the windows of heaven and bless them with a superabundance (see Malachi 3:8–10).

In the New Testament Paul expands this concept by saying that when we sow generously we will reap bountifully; when we give sparingly we receive a like measure in return. We are to give, not out of obligation or begrudgingly, but out of a joyful heart. "God loves a cheerful giver. And God is able to make all grace abound toward you, that you, always having all sufficiency in all things, may have an abundance for every good work" (2 Corinthians 9:7–8 NKJV). When we truly understand that everything we have is a gift from God (see James 1:17), and that apart from Him we can do absolutely nothing (see John 15:5), we will give out of love, not duty, and in proportion to what we have been given (see 1 Corinthians 16:2). As we bless the Lord with our giving, He blesses us.

My challenge to you is to pray before you give an offering or donate to charity. Ask God what would please Him and bring joy to His heart. Give generously and declare multiplication over your finances. Pray for expenses to decrease and income to increase.

Is Jesus master of your boat? Does He have permission to guide your career? Are you willing for Him to make changes in your life for His Kingdom purposes? If you are struggling to support yourself, have you thought of praying for creative sources of income?

Proverbs 8:12 says that with wisdom comes "knowledge of witty inventions" (KJV). Believers have received ideas for businesses and new products, often in a dream or in prayer. James 4:2 tells us: "You do not have because you do not ask God." James also cautions us to ask with godly motives, not greed or selfishness. Are you asking for creative ideas, favor at work, raises, bonuses and promotions? Are you taking the talents and resources that He has given you and using them for eternal purposes, or are you burying them in the ground for fear of losing them (see Matthew 25:15–30)?

Money miracles are awesome; however, I am not advocating irresponsible spending or presuming upon God to provide for your family while you twiddle your thumbs. His answer to financial needs may come in other forms—a new job, a promotion or starting a business. Divine provision is all about partnering with God to live life as He directs.

Ask God what His heart is for you and your family. When we are faithful in the area of finance, God releases abundance. Provision is a product of prayer, patience and partnering with Him. With obedience comes the supply for that which He calls you to do.

If the Lord challenges you with something that does not make sense in light of your finances, make sure to confirm it. Seek wise counsel if you are uncertain. But never let your lack keep you from obedience. Expect His supply to follow. God is just the same for spiritual superheroes as He is for those of us who live ordinary lives.

God is the source of our supply; this includes the time He gives us. Does time slip through your fingers? Is there a way to harness it for God's purposes? Let's find out.

Remember . . .

• When you depend on God for provision, you will see multiplication miracles.

• When you are faithful in even the smaller areas of finance, God releases abundance.

• Provision is a product of prayer, patience and partnering with Him.

• Are you taking the talents and resources that He has given you and using them for eternal purposes or burying them in the ground for fear of losing them?

17

Time Management

Praying about timing is an important part of our family's excursions. Our outing to Greenfield Village in Dearborn, Michigan, was no exception. Five of us packed into the car and headed for our destination four hours away.

"I'm fine with turning around and going home," my mother offered graciously after we had driven for an hour or so through torrential rain.

"Don't worry. We'll be fine," I replied calmly. *She probably thinks I'm crazy.* I had done due diligence, though. God had indicated it was the right day, which meant the weather would have to break at some point. Surely He would not send us to a historic village to walk around in the pouring rain. Yet the storm continued.

Shortly before our arrival, however, the downpour fizzled to a drizzle and finally exhausted itself. We enjoyed a wonderful day without a drop of rain. Relying on human reasoning would have caused us to turn the car around; prayer made all the difference.

God has individual plans and purposes for each of us. Psalm 139:16 says, "Your eyes saw my unformed body; all the days ordained for me were written in your book before one of them came to be." We each have our own God-written journals, spiritual daily planners that God prewrote before we were born. I do not obsess about every second; He probably did not write down "oatmeal" for breakfast today and "fish" for supper. But He does care about how we spend our time.

Do I pray about when to buy groceries? No. But my hairdresser does not take appointments, so I pray about what day and time to go. Sometimes God directs me to wait a day or tells me a specific time to be there. When I follow those directions I rarely ever wait more than a few minutes, if that. The last time I had to purchase tires, I prayed about the best day and time, knowing that one can wait for hours if the shop is busy. I followed God's directions and walked in right as the last two customers were leaving. The mechanics took my car right away.

God created us with unique gifts and talents. By ascertaining what is on His heart each morning, we give Him an opportunity to guide the use of our time and abilities more efficiently. While this may sound restrictive, it is actually liberating. Following His directives frees our time because we do not commit to time wasters. We all have important parts to play in God's plan for mankind. I do not want to miss any of it. Do you?

Personalities and Time Management

Our personalities can influence time management. Extroverts seem to collect people the way I collect books. They thrive on connecting with others. A response of yes might pop out of their mouths before giving an invitation much thought. But as one extroverted friend told me, "Good things are not always God things."

I prayed with an extroverted friend whose phone seemed to ring off the hook. She had more offers for lunch or coffee in one week than I had in months. She had a hard time saying no. The Lord showed me a picture of the enemy directing a stream of traffic toward her driveway, but Jesus had sent only a few visitors. Satan used those tempting invitations to distract her from God's plans. When she prayed and chose only those connections that God wanted her to keep, her phone stopped ringing incessantly, and she had more time to spend in prayer and the Word. Extroverts must guard against missing God's opportunities because they are busy elsewhere with "good" activities.

While extroverts have to rein in their readiness to say yes, introverts often have to be stretched out of their comfort zones. My default is no, so I must be careful to pray about opportunities that do not naturally appeal to me. By my doing so, God has directed me to pray in front of crowds and to attend gatherings and conferences that accomplish His purposes when I would prefer the quiet comfort of home. Conversely, I have learned to say no when pressured by a need for approval, obligation or guilt.

Then there are those who, like my daughter, are somewhere in the middle. She is not an extrovert, but she loves trying new things and volunteering. It is hard for her to pass up an opportunity to help someone. Please do not misunderstand. Helping people is godly, but she is not called to say yes to every opportunity. Learning to manage time means including God in our decisions so we are where He wants us to be, doing what He wants us to do.

Amelia was looking forward to the junior-senior banquet at her university but felt a check in her spirit about purchasing a ticket. It made no sense until afterward, when she heard all the negative reports about it from her fellow classmates. God had protected her from a dismal evening and saved her the cost of a dress and a $50 ticket.

We had the opportunity to spend a day at the beach toward the end of our first mission trip, but we had to sign up and pay for it a week in advance. In the natural I would have registered both kids since they love the ocean, but I prayed instead. I was surprised when the Lord said no. On the day of the beach excursion both kids were congested and exhausted and in no mood for a trip to the beach. They were content resting at the hotel all day, and I was grateful for the divine heads-up.

Whether we are extroverted, introverted or somewhere in between, it is wise to ask God if an open door is from Him or a distraction from what He wants us to do. This will help us avoid walking through open doors assuming it is a God-given opportunity, only to regret the choice later.

Whose Time Is It?

After reading *Cheaper by the Dozen* as a teenager, I wanted to be an efficiency expert just like the father in the story. I was fascinated by the thought of making the most of my time. As an adult, I have found that no matter how hard I try, my efforts fall far short of what God can accomplish through me when I commit my time to Him.

Over the years I have come to understand that our time belongs to the Lord, purchased on the cross by Christ's blood. Paul challenges us in Romans 12:1 to present ourselves as living sacrifices. Are we embracing all that God has planned for us, or squeezing Him in when it suits our needs?

Praying over your schedule may be a new concept, but if you struggle to find time to invest in the Lord and to read His Word daily, ask God what to keep and what to eliminate. Are God and your family your top priorities? Are you making commitments for activities that God directed you to, or did something else motivate you to sign up?

What about your family's schedule? Do your children's after-school and weekend commitments leave enough room for them to develop a personal relationship with the Lord? Is there enough margin in their schedules for family, developing their imaginations and down time? Praying about activities allows us an opportunity to hear God's heart on how we are spending our time and ensures that we are fulfilling our God-ordained destinies.

Now let's take stock for a moment. Are you feeling overwhelmed by the aspect of power praying? Are you saying to yourself at this point, *How am I going to do all of this?* Or maybe, *I don't seem to be hearing anything from God. Am I doing something wrong?* Don't be discouraged. It is time to turn the page.

Remember . . .

- God cares about how you spend your time, whether for leisure or work.

- Engaging God gives Him a chance to direct the use of your time and abilities more efficiently.
- Following His directives frees your time because you do not commit to time wasters.
- Are you embracing God's plans for you, or squeezing Him in when it suits your needs?

18

Discouraged but Not Defeated

The first time I picked up a tennis racket was my sophomore year in college. It took quite a bit of practice just to meet the ball in the center of the racket, let alone send it over the net. Hit then miss; hit then miss. Very few balls made it into the opposing court, but I kept at it. Hundreds (perhaps thousands) of hours of practice and many years later I competed in a few small tournaments. It was worth all the practice to arrive at that skill level.

Learning to put the power praying secrets into action—to hear God and follow His directives—is like that. It takes practice and determination. We have a need and start to wonder, *Which is the best way to pray?* We hear or see something as we sit and listen—and wonder again, *Is that really God or my imagination? Am I making all this up?*

I hope that the information in this book is helping you access God's wisdom in new and exciting ways. If, however, you are discouraged about how you will ever learn all that is taught here, remember that although it took me years and lots of trial and error to discover these secrets and keys, you will not have to go through the same discovery process. As I teach people how to connect with God, they pick it up rather quickly.

If you are discouraged because your attempts at hearing God have faltered, do not despair. In the beginning of my prayer journey I heard lots of silence and little to no God. Occasionally Scripture would come to mind or a word would appear printed in my mind's eye. I kept pressing in for more. "Lord, I really want to see pictures" became the cry of my heart for months. I figured that if I saw a picture I would know for sure it was God, but I questioned the pictures when they eventually came. After much exasperation I decided to trust more, doubt less and test what I was receiving.

Much of my frustration came from listening in my head and not my heart. I had to stop analyzing and start receiving by faith in my spirit. Now when I listen, I focus on the Lord, not my situation. Once an image or impression comes I ask Him to repeat it or confirm it in a different way if it is from Him or erase it if it is not. This has increased my confidence in recognizing how the Lord speaks to me.

We must overcome our fear of making mistakes in order to fine tune our listening skills. The riches of God's wisdom are available for the asking. Because He chooses to partner with us to accomplish His plans on earth, He is patient while we learn. It takes years of investing money to see a substantial return, yet we cannot take it with us when we die. Our investment in learning to hear God, however, will last for eternity.

If you have not already done this, create a strong foundation by asking for passion to pursue Him and for intense hunger for His Word. Passion and hunger will jump-start your spiritual battery every morning. Without them it is harder to persevere when you hit pockets of silence.

Guard against discouragement by working on one secret at a time. Practice it when praying for simple, low-risk decisions first. Slowly work your way up to asking about more complicated issues as you gain confidence in your ability to hear God. Commit your decisions to Him, but recognize that it will take much practice before you are hearing accurately on a consistent basis.

We are warned not to despise small beginnings (see Zechariah 4:10), so giving thanks for any progress is important. Celebrate successes. Redeem mistakes by asking God what went wrong. Focus on increasing accuracy, not on perfection.

My mistake level dropped dramatically when I sought confirmations consistently and when I established spiritual parameters to block Satan's lies and deceptions. When asking for wisdom, I prefer to pray silently. As I have mentioned, this prevents the kingdom of darkness from overhearing what I am seeking the Lord about and from substituting a deceptive answer. It is one more level of protection from enemy interference.

My goal is to catch discouragement as soon as it pops into my mind. I give it to the Lord, ask Him to replace it with His peace and ask Him to tell me His truth about my situation. If I hear nothing, I read Scripture out loud from the encouraging verses I have written on index cards. One of my favorites is this: "For with God nothing is ever impossible and *no word from God shall be without power* or impossible of fulfillment" (Luke 1:37 AMPLIFIED, emphasis added). That assures me that His promises to me contain the power to manifest if I hold on to and declare them with faith. I also thank the Lord for His wisdom and declare His ability to use every situation for good (see Romans 8:28), no matter what it appears like in the natural.

Remember the ten spies who disagreed with God's assurance that the Promised Land would be theirs? "They were not able to enter, because of their unbelief" (Hebrews 3:19). Like Joshua's and Caleb's, our words must agree with God's plan—even if it looks impossible—or we risk losing God's promise to us.

When our daughter's college application was rejected, we were careful not to say anything contrary to God's plans for her. While we battled discouragement over the next seven months (not knowing how or when God would get her in), I continued to declare that she would attend. Doubt plays into the enemy's hand, so I avoided making statements like "Well, you might not get in." This was not superstitious behavior, but a testimony to our belief in God's faithfulness and His ability to do what seemed impossible. Confident declarations affirm our belief in what God has shown us and strengthen our faith.

I declare God's promises out loud in my private prayer time, but I use discretion about sharing them publicly. Unless I feel led to make a statement of faith, I generally avoid unnecessary confrontation with naysayers. It is important to maintain an attitude of faith while waiting to see God's promises fulfilled.

Jesus healed the centurion's servant when He heard the centurion express his belief in Christ's ability to heal (see

Matthew 8:5–13). Will He see faith in how we act and speak? It might seem as though we are talking nonsense if what we declare flies in the face of what we see, but that is exactly the steadfast belief that God is looking for—faith to believe the impossible, faith that waits for miracles, faith that states boldly that Christ is Lord over our circumstances. God specializes in the impossible; consequently, He alone receives the credit.

I am not advocating making a wish list and calling it into being as if reciting a magical incantation. Presumption is deciding your own agenda and declaring it. Discovering God's heart and His blueprint for your life is the key. It is what you receive from God's heart that you declare to your circumstances and into the atmosphere around you. It is *His* plan, not ours, that we testify to, regardless of what our current situations look like. Our faith declarations demonstrate our intention to follow His timetable and His agenda, not ours.

In 2 Corinthians 4:18 we are advised to concentrate on the invisible things of God, for they are eternal, rather than the visible things of this world, which are temporary and subject to change. Rather than focusing on discouraging circumstances, we need to partner with God to change those circumstances by believing in and declaring the revelations He gives us when we listen to His heart.

I spent years operating solely from my own talents. Because I was not intentionally pursuing God's plan for my life, I was unconsciously cooperating with the enemy. My lukewarmness toward the Lord was Satan's plan for me—my self-determination and self-fulfillment subtly playing into the enemy's hand. Transitioning from self-reliance to dependence on God feels uncomfortable at first, but it is the only way to see supernatural answers to prayers. Ask for His mercy and grace to undergird you as you allow Him to call the shots rather than striving in your own strength.

Have you ever felt at your wit's end and unable even to pray? That is when breath prayers come in handy—short phrases such as these:

I trust You.

You are my strength.

Pull me through this, Lord.

Give me wisdom, Father.

Repeating one or more of them saturates my soul and strengthens my spirit. In times of desperation, I also ask God to dispatch His ministering angels to comfort and strengthen me (see Matthew 4:11).

The enemy loves to delay the answers to our prayers in order to discourage and wear us out (see Daniel 10:2–13). Rather than giving up and blaming God for not answering, let 1 John 5:14–15 bring reassurance: "This is the confidence we have in approaching God: that if we ask anything according to his will, he hears us. And if we know that he hears us—whatever we ask—we know that we have what we asked of him." If I am praying what God has revealed to me, that verse helps me stay the course, knowing the answer will eventually come.

When discouraged be careful to keep your thoughts on God, stay in the present moment and guard against fear of the future. God holds your future in His hands. It might help to review your prayer journal, remembering how faithful God has already been. You might also take your mind off the circumstances by doing something creative, taking a walk or listening to praise music. Remember, God created the universe out of what is invisible to us. In the same way He can create a solution to your problem from what you are not yet able to see.

Some people have comfort food. I have comfort books. In times of despair I can turn to any page in Hannah Whitall Smith's book *The God of All Comfort* and find encouragement. *Just Enough Light for the Step I'm On* by Stormie Omartian and *Be Anxious for Nothing* by Joyce Meyer are other standbys. These women have experienced considerable suffering and know how to comfort and encourage.

God wants us to persevere; Satan wants us to quit. How different our world would look if inventors and manufacturers gave up after a few unsuccessful attempts at a new product! We cannot let failures and mistakes keep us from learning to hear God and accessing His divine wisdom and praying with power. Proverbs 24:16 encourages me when I mess up: "For a righteous man falls seven times and rises again" (AMPLIFIED). Pick yourself up, dust yourself off and try again.

The advice in this book is not meant to be a formula, but a guide to a soul-satisfying spiritual connection with our Lord. Keep your relationship with the Lord the main focus, and remember that God longs to communicate His heart to you. God will never quit on you or bail out of the relationship. You can have as much of Him as you are willing to invest in pursuing Him. It is a winning proposition.

Now if you think you *have* made a mistake, your journey in learning to hear God is not over. This is the subject of our next chapter.

Remember . . .

- Guard against discouragement by working on the seven secrets one at a time. Practice when praying for simple, low-risk decisions first.

- God can create a solution to your problem from what you are not yet able to see.

- Keep your thoughts on God, stay in the present moment and guard against fear of the future.

- Are you willing to stay the course? You cannot lose if you do not quit.

19

Learning from Mistakes

I was seventeen and enjoying my first meal with the French family with whom I would be living for the summer. Unused to large, multicourse meals, my stomach said enough after the soup and salad. How could I refuse the third course without appearing rude to my hosts? Leaning over to my French "sister," I whispered, "I'm full," in my best French. Her eyes widened and then she giggled. I just made my first faux pas. My faulty English-to-French translation came out as an idiom meaning "I am pregnant."

Learning to listen to God can be like that: Something gets lost in the translation, and we make an embarrassing error or, possibly worse, an error in judgment. All the more reason to seek confirmations, especially in important decisions. When in doubt, continue seeking the Lord and mature, godly counsel.

We are exhorted in 1 Thessalonians 5:21 not to accept all things as coming from God, but to test and prove everything.

When we approach God with a humble, teachable heart, He will show us His truth (see Psalm 25:9). Flubbing is not fun. Like my gracious French "sister," we need to show grace to ourselves and others when this happens. Mistakes are temporary. Learning to hear God will last a lifetime. I hope that understanding these seven common errors will help you to avoid them.

Mistake #1: A Fixed Mindset

When my ten-year-old car "died" in an accident, I enlisted a friend to help me shop for a replacement. I questioned her guidance, however, when she announced, "*Top of the line. That's what God told me when I prayed about a car for you.*"

Had God forgotten our income? We could not afford top of the line. She must have heard wrong.

"Show us your top of the line," my friend told the salesman at the car dealership. His eyes popped with dollar signs, while I was busy telling God we could not afford it. I had intended to start searching at the *bottom* of the line.

Early in life I learned to count the cost of any purchase. Because we had to scrimp and save during those years, I came to doubt that God wanted to bless me materially. I always looked for the cheapest sale and the best bargains. Thus, as the salesman led my friend toward new top-of-the-line models, I hurried to correct them. "I think we need to look at the economy models," I said.

Many test drives later I thought I had found the perfect choice. My brother owned the same model car I was considering, and while visiting him, I had the opportunity to drive his car for three hours. That is when I discovered that the lack of lumbar support gave me a backache. My husband made the final decision: "You need the more expensive model." We ended up with an affordable three-year-old top-of-the-line car, and my back has thanked me for it.

A fixed mindset can block or distort our hearing from God. When we have not dealt with our personal biases, we may not be open to God's best for us. I made two mistakes when looking for a new car. First, I failed to ask God if He had any advice for me. Second, based on my bias, I assumed that less expensive models were my only option. Had I sought confirmation instead of automatically brushing off what my friend heard from God, I would have saved lots of time.

When praying about decisions, here are some questions to ask: Am I restricting God's hands by setting a deadline for His answer? Am I open to whatever the Lord directs me to do? Am I willing to wait on His timing?

Strong negative opinions (such as "I could never . . .") and lack of flexibility are red flags that personal prejudice might be operating in our lives. The more we identify and eliminate biases, the easier it becomes to align our thoughts and hearts with God's plan for us.

Mistake #2: Yielding to Fear

Three common fears can derail our ability to make decisions with God at the center: fear of making mistakes, fear of man and fear of the cost.

One Sunday I prayed with a friend for guidance. While God did not reveal what I needed to do, He directed her to say: "Trust that God will correct you if you are making a mistake or heading in the wrong direction." God nailed the issue. I had succumbed to fear of making a mistake. That fear blocked my ability to move forward. God wanted to deal with the fear first so I could trust that He would guide me in His timing.

King Saul gave in to the fear of man. Instead of destroying all the Amalekites and the spoils as the Lord commanded, he and the Israelites saved the best of the plunder and spared the Amalekite king. When confronted by Samuel, Saul admitted that he had disobeyed the Lord. "I have sinned. I violated the LORD's command and your instructions. I was afraid of the men and so I gave in to them" (1 Samuel 15:24). It cost Saul his kingdom. How many of us have made poor decisions because we allowed ourselves to be swayed by what our fellow man might think instead of listening to the Lord?

Fear of what it will cost to obey God, whether time or money, can also block us from receiving His directives. Through our intimate relationship with God and listening to His heart, His will is revealed to us. When we obey His revealed will, we have the abundant life that Jesus promised (see John 10:10).

The summer that God told me to take the kids for a mini-vacation to Moravian Falls I struggled with fear of what it would cost. An Internet search revealed a reasonably priced cabin, but I fretted about sending in the $100 down payment. What if God did not provide? After multiple confirmations to go ahead, I finally mailed the deposit, but I could not share the children's excitement about spending two days in the mountains. We needed $300. Where would we get it?

With only three weeks left, I pressed in for the specifics of financing this excursion. As I sat quietly focusing on God, He reminded me of a recent chat with a bank teller who mentioned something about a rewards program. A call to the bank confirmed I had enough points to redeem for $200 cash. The biggest shock came the following week when I received an envelope containing $100 in cash and an unsigned note that read simply, "Thank you." Our faith skyrocketed. By packing our own food, we had enough money to pay for the retreat.

God is able to call "those things which do not exist as though they did" (Romans 4:17 NKJV). We must be careful not to let a bank balance drown out God's voice. If we fail to believe that He can provide what we do not have, we may miss divine opportunities. He can create new jobs, prosper a business and multiply finances. Learning to trust God in money matters takes practice, but God will supply the training experiences if we seek and obey His will first.

Mistake #3: Ignoring Nudges and Checks

My mother and daughter were flying to visit my brother in North Carolina. Amelia parked the car in long-term parking. Since the weather was clear and they would be gone only three days, Grandma decided to leave her raincoat on the backseat. Amelia felt an impression to bring the coat, but Grandma insisted she would not need it. When it came time to take her medication later that evening, my mother realized that her pills were left behind in the pocket of her raincoat. It took fast footwork to get her prescriptions replaced at a pharmacy just minutes before closing time. Amelia learned an important lesson that day: Obey nudges in spite of resistance.

The kids were in elementary school when I discovered an engaging hands-on devotional workbook for families. As I walked excitedly downstairs to gather the crew, I sensed an inner tugging in my spirit to wait. *What could possibly be wrong with doing a devotional?* I thought and forged ahead.

Within minutes I found myself in a verbal sparring match. It was a disaster. My agenda was not in sync with God's timing.

The temptation to ignore checks and nudges usually comes when we are tired, impatient or do not want to be inconvenienced. But paying attention to those nudges and checks can spare us disastrous consequences.

Mistake #4: Substituting Man's Advice for God's Will

My friend Samantha struggled in a difficult marriage for years. Each time a friend advised her to leave, she sought the Lord's wisdom and received another promise of reconciliation. Had she taken her friends' counsel instead of trusting what God said, she would not have seen her marriage restored more than ten years later.

A word about unusual directives from God: If they contradict common sense, naysayers will play devil's advocate. Jesus told the ruler of the synagogue to ignore the report that his daughter had died and to keep on believing as they walked to his house. Jesus kept the doubters outside while He took the parents and three disciples in to where the little girl lay and raised her from the dead (see Mark 5:35–43).

Well-intended but erroneous comments, if not deflected by faith, can derail us from obeying the Lord. We must not shift our eyes from the Lord's plan or give in to the fear of losing someone's approval. Following God is not a forty-yard dash but more like a steeplechase—jumping ditches and fences and avoiding obstacles as we head toward the finish line. Make sure you confirm what you hear and that it does not violate Scripture. Ultimately we answer to God alone for all our decisions.

Mistake #5: Quitting at the First Hurdle

In Secret #6 we learned how to use power praying to open locked doors. Sometimes, however, we are so overwhelmed with obstacles that we want to quit. Quitting too soon is such a common mistake that I want to discuss it here.

Have you ever watched athletes run hurdles? They never take their eyes off the finish line even when they knock a hurdle over. When we face an obstacle that seems too high to jump, it is not the time to quit. It is time to ask, What's next, Lord?

My daughter's trip to Mozambique provided numerous opportunities to quit. Not only was the first flight canceled at 5:30 a.m. Friday, but the rescheduled departure at 2:30 p.m. and then at 6:00 p.m. were delayed as well. I had already started driving home when she called to inform me of the latest glitch. I pulled off the highway to pray.

"Lord, what do You want to show us about this situation?" With bruised shins we hit this third hurdle ready to throw in the towel. I asked God to quiet our emotions. Within a short while an image of breadcrumbs winding in a line off into the distance appeared in my mind.

"Amelia, God wants you to follow the breadcrumbs." A short summary of the Hansel and Gretel fairy tale cleared up the analogy for her. God's breadcrumbs would lead Amelia step by step to her final destination. Her flight began boarding as we ended the prayer, only to be delayed again before finally taking off. It would not be the last of the breadcrumbs.

The next morning Amelia called numerous times from London about difficulties with her connecting flights. After we straightened those out, her London flight was pushed back four hours, threatening to undo all the rebooking and strand her in Nairobi, Kenya. We bombarded heaven with prayer until God's breadcrumbs brought her safely to Mozambique Sunday afternoon.

If you have tried accessing God's heart but do not feel as though you have connected personally with Him yet, do not give up. God wants you more than you want Him. You are His child. He loves you more than you love yourself. Quitting will not accomplish anything; it will only cause you to sink slowly into spiritual mediocrity. Determine to stir up your inner man to run hard after God. Remember, the Word says that you will find Him when you seek Him with all of your heart (not your head). Invest your energy in the One who will satisfy your soul with love, joy, peace, patience and all the benefits of being intimately connected to your Creator.

In the midst of pursuing God's plans for our lives we may knock over some hurdles, but by God's grace we can still finish the race. We cannot lose if we do not quit.

Mistake #6: Taking Control

Life would be so much easier if all we needed was our own personal game controller. Push this button and explode our problems; twist the joystick and avoid a catastrophe. In reality, however, life flows smoother when we relinquish control to God.

Trying to call all the shots can lead to disastrous results. The Lord had promised Abraham and Sarah a child, but after ten years of waiting Sarah decided to take matters into her own hands. Ishmael, the child of Sarah's maid, was not God's promised heir.

In contrast, David, even though anointed by Samuel to be king of Israel, refused to take control of the throne prematurely. He passed up two opportunities to kill Saul, trusting

God to establish him on the throne in His own timing (see 1 Samuel 24:6; 26:11).

God showed a friend of mine a picture of what happens when we try to control matters. Imagine a clear piece of tubing as the channel through which the Holy Spirit flows into our lives to guide and direct us. When we try to control the outcome, it is as if we squeeze the tube until nothing can pass through, thus blocking God's best for us.

When tempted to take matters into our own hands, we need to let go of the outcome and simply ask God, "Is there anything You want me to do right now?," then follow His promptings. If He does not direct us specifically, then, like David, we need to trust God to orchestrate the end results, remembering that God is wise enough and powerful enough to manage our situations better than we can.

Mistake #7: Focusing on Our Own Weaknesses

Some of God's assignments stretch me far beyond my natural abilities, like the time we were scheduled to do street ministry on our mission trip to Rio de Janeiro. I put on my shoes that morning, but someone had nailed them to the floor. Or so I thought. Paralyzing fear overcame me. How could I talk to strangers about Christ? Yet I knew it was God's heart for me that day. "God, I simply cannot do this. You will have to help me move my feet forward. *Please.*"

Others had done this and survived. Determined to obey the Lord, I shut the door on introspection and focused on His power. As I did, the paralysis lifted. That afternoon I discovered that I can truly do all things through Christ. God demonstrates His strength most effectively in our weaknesses (see 2 Corinthians 12:9). Street ministry was the highlight of that trip: I led two teenagers in a prayer of salvation and prayed for several others with physical or emotional problems.

What we focus on becomes our reality. I wasted many hours telling God how big my problems were and how inadequate I was to handle them, when I should have been telling myself how mighty God is. Rather than cave in to our weaknesses and miss God's blessings, we need to tune in to our identity in Christ. Christ in us is sufficient for every situation and every decision.

"As for God, his way is perfect: The LORD's word is flawless; he shields all who take refuge in him" (Psalm 18:30). In the process of learning to trust God, His timing, His strength and His wisdom, mistakes are inevitable. Equally inescapable, however, is His love, forgiveness and grace. You may get egg on your face, but be patient. It takes time and persistence to learn how to access God's heart and follow His divine directives. It is a learning curve; we all start at the bottom and learn our way up. We must continue to press in, press on and press upward.

It is almost time to close the book, but first we must know how to close the gap.

Remember . . .

- Confirm what you hear and make sure that it does not violate Scripture.
- Quitting will not accomplish anything; it will only cause you to slowly sink into spiritual mediocrity.
- Avoid telling God (and others) how big your problems are. Tell yourself how big God is.
- Are you willing to let go of the outcome and let God guide you with His divine directives?

20

Close the Gap

Let's do an experiment. Put your right hand, thumb up, in front of you. This represents God. Now place your left hand (which represents you) parallel to your right. Move your hands together or apart to symbolize how close to God or how far from God you feel right now. Are your hands inches apart, a foot apart or stretched as far apart you can reach?

Is the space a crevice or a chasm? That is the gap God wants to close. Why? God's primary desire is a tight-knit relationship with us. He created us for daily companionship, as He did Adam and Eve. Without an intimate relationship with God, we will neglect to keep Him in the center of our lives. And when we sideline God, we miss opportunities to use the secrets to power praying and miss accessing God's wisdom—and miracles—every day.

What Creates the Gap?

Raised in a denominational church, I grew up with head knowledge rather than heart knowledge of God. I had no idea He wanted to connect with anyone, let alone me. If you had asked me where God lived, I would have pointed to the farthest galaxy in the universe, and that was *after* being confirmed in the church. He was distant and austere. The gap between God and me back then was farther than my arms could stretch.

A distorted concept of God creates a gulf between us and Him. He may seem critical, aloof or a spoilsport if we did not have a loving (or any) relationship with an earthly father. Unfortunately, God's PR men and women are often other Christians who also feel distant from their heavenly Father. The absence of that heart connection makes it easy to walk away from God or pocket Him into a small corner of our lives. What we believe about God determines our approach to power praying.

Although I had eliminated God from the time line of my life during college and premed postgraduate studies, He had not crossed me off His Most Wanted List. When I was applying for medical school, God used an interview with an actor on a television talk show to grab my attention. As I watched Pat Boone radiate a captivating joy and peace that I had never known, I wondered, *Where did he get that?* I had to know the source. Maybe his book, *A New Song*, would tell me. In the middle of reading how Christ changed his life, I heard an inner audible voice make one compelling statement: *Choose today whom you will serve.* Ignoring the challenge to jump off the spiritual fence I was sitting on, I turned back to my reading. God shook the fence again, giving me no rest until I answered.

"I'll get religious when I'm older," I said to no one in particular. "I want control of my life—and I don't want to go to church."

Choose today whom you will serve was the only reply to my rebellious retort. Laying the book on my chest, I pondered my choices. All of creation points to a Creator, so I had no problem believing in God. But what about Jesus? He claimed to be the Son of God who sacrificed His life to pay for my sins and to give me eternal life. By not choosing Christ as my Savior, I realized that I was choosing to serve Satan by default (see John 3:18). I had never thought of it that way.

There would be no middle ground after I died; I would be either in or out of heaven, either for God or against Him. I realized my feet were not planted on the Rock of Jesus Christ but on Satan's quicksand. I recommitted my life to Christ, and the enemy's invisible net of deception released my soul and my future. I began to experience God in ways I would not have expected. I found a Bible, read a few sentences and sensed the words were alive. *Who rewrote this book?* I wondered. In reality, God had rewritten my heart.

Convicted that my worldly reasons for applying to medical school fell far short of godly motives, I surrendered the application process to God and asked Him to make it clear if He wanted me to proceed. I had no idea how He would show me. I just knew I could not attend med school if it was not His will.

Shortly thereafter on a Monday morning, I began to hear an inner voice telling me, *Call the admissions office. They will tell you that you have been accepted.* It made no sense since I had been told that the admissions committee would meet on Wednesday, but the sentence kept repeating. I did not fully comprehend that it was actually God speaking to me, but to silence the persistent voice, I called the admissions office. The secretary asked if I had checked my mail that day. No, I had not.

"You'll find your acceptance letter in your mailbox," she informed me. I was stunned. Indeed, the letter had already arrived.

Unfortunately, despite other supernatural experiences in the months that followed (like finding the missing contact lens), the intensity of medical school, residency, a new career and a family left little time for God. Although I attended church weekly and prayed regularly, I did not understand God's desire for a deeply personal relationship, that I would have to carve out time intentionally to experience more of Him and His miraculous nature. Even after discovering how amazing God is, I allowed my hectic schedule to silence His voice. It took that malpractice suit to catapult me into His presence.

Busyness is not the only thing that drives a wedge between us and God. Distractions, sin and unforgiveness can create a chasm, too. Do we make time for the morning paper but not the Word? Are we more worried about our investments than investing ourselves in Him? Is holding a grudge against a family member really worth compromising our relationship with the Lord? When we turn down our thermostats, our homes cool off; when we decrease our time with God, our love for Him cools off.

Satan's goal is to jam his foot into the space between us and God. Just as he sowed seeds of doubt in Eve, he plants questions in our thoughts that undermine God's Word and His character. The enemy of our souls slips stealthily into that gap and widens the distance by stealing our time with

God, focusing our attention on material things or derailing us with pride, greed, lust, etc. If Satan wins our minds by creating doubt, unbelief or lukewarmness, he wins the spoils.

Although the malpractice suit initially turned my life upside down, God meant it for good (see Genesis 50:20). Even before the case was dropped, I was able to thank the Lord for using it to breathe spiritual hunger, maturity and discipline into my life.

Drawing His Presence

James 4:8 gives us a clue to closing the gap: "Come near to God and he will come near to you." Praise and passion draw His presence. Psalm 22:3 tells us that He inhabits the praises of His people. If you do not enjoy singing your praises, then listening to praise music and worshiping Him through declarations out loud or in your thoughts enables you to experience Him just as much as singing does. Hanging around other believers who are on fire for God can kick-start passion to draw close to Him if our spiritual temperature is lukewarm. Whatever means we choose, as we move closer to Him, He will move toward us.

I can almost hear someone say, "But you don't understand. I really don't have a minute to myself all week." Let's see, what about your coffee break, or part of your lunch hour, or even a bathroom break? Surely there are ten or fifteen minutes when you could wholeheartedly pursue God each day (or multiple times a day). Invite the Holy Spirit to permeate your office each morning with His presence or to fill the atmosphere of your car as you commute or run errands. Express your gratitude to Him while mowing the lawn. If you are waiting in line at the bank or filling your tank at the pump you have time to pray, "Lord, I need Your presence right now. Fill me afresh with Your Spirit."

Why not take a few minutes right now to thank Him for your life, your family, your health and all the other blessings He has given you. If your passion has waned, ask Him to stir up a fire in your heart for Him.

The Lord longs to spend time with you. He looks forward to your presence every day. You are the desire of His heart. God cannot resist passionate people. If we can stir up fervor about a basketball game, can we not do the same for Him?

Soaking Prayer

We cannot stand still and stay with God. If we do not continually make strides toward Him we will begin to backslide. Relationships progress by moving forward; they are dynamic, not static. I want as much of God as I can pack into my lifetime. Once you have tasted His presence you will see it is *the* most exciting part of life.

If you are serious about experiencing more of God's limitless nature, then "soaking prayer" is your answer. Carve out thirty to sixty minutes to be alone with Him and express your heartfelt desire: "God, I want more of You. I want to feel Your presence. Fill me with Your love." Repeat those words as if your life depended on them, then simply rest as you focus on the Lord. Resist the urge to talk about problems. Relax and train your thoughts on Christ. Some Christian recording artists, like John Belt, produce soothing music that is conducive to soaking. The more you urge your spirit to connect with the Lord, the more it will become compelling, the more you will hunger for His presence and the more you will make certain you find time to soak.

Soaking in the Lord builds a positive balance in our spiritual bank accounts that we can draw upon later. A day or two after immersing in His presence, I often experience a supernatural demonstration of His love or power. Those who radiate the love of Christ saturate themselves in that love on a regular basis. Find time this week to devote solely to pursuing God's company. When you have experienced His tangible presence, you will not want to live without it.

When God Creates the Gap

Will we always feel close to God? No, there are seasons when we have done everything right, but God seems to vanish into thin air. If we ask the Holy Spirit to search our souls and nothing is amiss, it might be that God has moved down the hallway, so to speak, to wait for us in another room. He wants us to follow Him to a higher level of spiritual maturity or to experience a new aspect of His nature.

Are we hungry enough to pursue Him no matter where He leads? Will we keep seeking Him even if it takes longer than we would like to feel His presence again? "You will seek me and find me when you seek me with all your heart" (Jeremiah 29:13). If you are in one of these dry seasons, it helps to remember these truths:

God always wants good for us (see Jeremiah 29:11; Lamentations 3:25).

He is always with us (see Matthew 28:20).

He will give us peace as we focus on and hope in Him (see Isaiah 26:3).

When we call, He promises to answer (see Jeremiah 33:3). He promises to give us wisdom if we ask in faith (see James 1:5–8).

You are the only one who can decide to draw closer to God. It does not depend on anyone else. I do not have all the answers, but my daily goal is to engage with the One who does. You can have all the money in the world and not have God. Conversely, you can have nothing the world values and have all of God that you desire simply by pursuing and embracing His presence. His offer is so lopsided! All the riches of His wisdom are ours simply by drawing close and asking.

The Challenge

Every morning when you get up, place your hands in that same position and ask yourself, *How close am I to God right now, and how close do I want to be to Him at the end of my day?* I challenge you to make Him a priority on a daily basis.

Supernatural answers to prayer are all about Him—glorifying His name and making Him personal to others. Anything that you can possibly dream of for yourself pales in comparison to God's plans for you. You cannot be perfect, but inwardly and outwardly are you pursuing Him passionately? Is your heart's desire to live a life pleasing to Him? Will your tomorrow be different from today by implementing what you have just learned? Are you anchored to His plans or drifting on the cultural tide around you?

God is looking for His people to be marathoners, not sprinters. If you have sprinted before and dropped out of the race, it is never too late to jump back in. My prayer for you is that you partner with God fully in your prayer life so that you become a living testimony of His miracle-working power.

Life with God is exciting when He is at the center. As Randy Clark says, "There's always more of Him. *Press in.*"

Challenge yourself to take the plunge. God's solutions to your problems are priceless, yet free. Your own supernatural answers are waiting to be released!

Remember . . .

- Draw near to God through praise and worship, and He will draw near to you.
- You cannot stand still and stay close to God. You must continually move toward Him.
- Soaking in God's presence enables you to radiate His love to those around you.
- How close are you to the Lord right now? What will you do to close the gap?

Appendix A

Power Prayers and Declarations

The following prayers and declarations are some of the ones that have been the most powerful for me. Some have already been mentioned in the text, but I have categorized them here for convenience.

Wisdom

Lord, release Your Spirit of truth, wisdom, revelation, knowledge and wise counsel to me.

Align my thoughts to agree with Your thoughts and my heart to agree with Your heart.

Flood the eyes of my heart to see Your truth.

I commit this problem to You. I trust that You will act in Your timing.

Let me see this situation (or person) through the eyes of Your Holy Spirit.

Is there anything else I need to know before making this decision?

Send forth Your light and truth to lead and guide me.

Health

In the name of Jesus, I bind all spirits of infirmity and affliction and command them to leave my body immediately and not to return or to send others in their places.

My body is the temple of the Holy Spirit. It is off limits to any illness or infirmity.

I am one with Christ in body, mind and spirit, and sickness has no dominion over me. It must leave.

I command all lying signs and symptoms to leave my body and not return, in Jesus' name.

Lord, send the river of life into our home; wherever the river flows it brings healing and restoration.

My family is prospering and in good health, just as our souls prosper.

Home

I release the Kingdom of God into my home—life, peace, health, love, hope and joy.

Lord, love my family through me. Be patient through me today.

In Jesus' name I bind all spirits of division, strife and disunity. I release a spirit of unity into the atmosphere of my home.

I cover the doorposts of my home, my family and our possessions with the blood of the Lamb.

Lord, hide my family under the shelter of Your wings.

Lord, I take refuge in You. Be a wall of heavenly fire around my family.

Lord, command Your angels to protect my family.

No weapon forged against my family will prosper.

I am an overcomer. Anoint my family with the oil of the overcomer.

Lord, please remove any obstacles or roadblocks the enemy would try to put in my family's path today.

Finances

Lord, bless me to be a blessing to others.

Multiply our family's finances thirty, sixty, a hundredfold.

Give our family a Kingdom mentality for being good stewards of our finances.

Cause the work of my hands to prosper.

Create multiple supply lines.

Give me a Kingdom mindset and generous heart to steward what You have given me.

Appendix B

Attributes of God

For a mind that is peaceful and trusts God, focus on His nature and attributes:

Our Shepherd

Our Comforter

Our Provision

Our Righteousness

King of kings, Lord of lords

Ruler and Creator of the universe

Our Redeemer

Our Friend

Our Defense in all circumstances

Our Counselor

Our Wisdom

Our Advocate

All-wise

All-powerful

All-knowing

All-present

Our Refuge

Our Strength

Our Protector

Our Deliverer

Our Healer

Our Peace

Our Sure Foundation

Our Guide

Full of grace

Giver of good gifts

Author of our salvation

Our Father

Everything we need for every situation

Faithful to His Word

A Promise Keeper

The Lifter of our heads

Appendix C

Suggested Reading

Beale, Adrian and Adam F. Thompson. *The Divinity Code*. Richmond, South Australia: Hyde Park Press, 2009.

Blackaby, Henry T. and Claude V. King. *Experiencing God*. Nashville: LifeWay Press, 1990.

Blackaby, Henry and Melvin. *Experiencing the Spirit: The Power of Pentecost Every Day*. Colorado Springs: Multnomah, 2009.

Dawson, Joy. *The Fire of God*. Shippensburg, Penn.: Destiny Image, 2005.

———. *Forever Ruined for the Ordinary*. Nashville: Thomas Nelson, 2001.

———. *Intimate Friendship with God*. Grand Rapids: Chosen, 2008.

Deere, Jack. *Surprised by the Voice of God*. Grand Rapids: Zondervan, 1998.

Hogue, Rodney. *Forgiveness*. Hayward, Calif.: Rodney Hogue, 2008.

Ibojie, Joe. *Illustrated Dictionary of Dream Symbols: A Biblical Guide to Your Dreams and Visions*. Shippensburg, Penn.: Destiny Image, 2010.

Idleman, Kyle. *Not a Fan*. Grand Rapids: Zondervan, 2011.

Jacobs, Cindy. *The Voice of God*. Ventura, Calif.: Regal, 2004.

Kreider, Larry. *Hearing God 30 Different Ways*. Lititz, Penn.: House to House Publications, 2006.

———. *Speak, Lord, I'm Listening*. Ventura, Calif.: Regal, 2008.

Lord, Peter. *Hearing God: An Easy-to-Follow, Step-by-Step Guide to Two-Way Communication with God*. Grand Rapids: Chosen, 2011.

Meyer, Joyce. *Battlefield of the Mind*. New York: Warner Faith, 1995.

———. *Be Anxious for Nothing: The Art of Casting Your Cares and Resting in God*. New York: FaithWords, 2002.

Milligan, Ira. *The Ultimate Guide to Understanding the Dreams You Dream: Biblical Keys for Hearing God's Voice in the Night*. Shippensburg, Penn.: Treasure House, 2012.

Omartian, Stormie. *Just Enough Light for the Step I'm On: Trusting God in the Tough Times*. Eugene, Ore.: Harvest House, 2008.

Sheets, Dutch. *Authority in Prayer*. Minneapolis: Bethany, 2007.

Smith, Hannah Whitall. *The God of All Comfort*. Uhrichsville, Oh.: Barbour, 1984.

Trimm, Cindy. *Commanding Your Morning: Unleash the Power of God in Your Life*. Lake Mary, Fla.: Charisma, 2007.

Jane Glenchur, M.D., never intended to go into medicine. She studied French and spent a summer living in France to develop fluency in the language before changing her major and graduating from Indiana University with a B.A. in speech pathology and audiology.

She has a master's degree in audiology from the University of Louisville, where she taught as a clinical instructor in audiology for five years in their graduate speech and hearing program. Her passion to learn led her to enroll in evening law school. During this time in her career as an audiologist she was assigned to perform hearing evaluations at the University Hospital Otolaryngology Clinic. Working with hospital patients and medical residents ignited a passion for medicine. She finished a semester of law school and immediately enrolled in evening premed classes for the next two years prior to being admitted to the University of Louisville School of Medicine.

She completed a six-month internship in internal medicine and a year of pathology training before completing her dermatology residency and dermatopathology fellowship at the University of Cincinnati.

As a board-certified dermatologist and dermatopathologist, Dr. Glenchur worked for eight years in a private group practice, seeing patients and diagnosing biopsies and surgical specimens, before being called to be a stay-at-home mom.

Dr. Glenchur served in numerous volunteer capacities at the Christian college prep academy her children attended, in addition to being an active participant in the mothers' intercessory prayer group for ten years. She stepped down from her leadership role in the prayer group to serve on their board of trustees for the past four years.

She has been a team leader on multiple Youth Power Invasion mission trips to Brazil with Randy Clark and Global Awakening. As a result of these mission trips she is passionate about praying for physical and inner healing and loves serving as a spiritual mentor especially to young adults. She was recently invited to serve as a medical associate for the Global Medical Research Institute, which was begun by Randy Clark for the purpose of documenting medical miracles.

Prayer is Dr. Glenchur's number one passion and as such she is active in several intercessory prayer groups. She has taught a number of Bible studies and is passionate about teaching others to hear God and involve Him in their decision making.

When she is not writing or reading, she enjoys creating handcrafted greeting cards and playing with the family's Maltese dog and pet flying squirrel. She and her husband, Tom, have two children and live in Ohio.

If you are interested in inviting Dr. Glenchur to speak, please contact her at janeglenchur@gmail.com.

Follow her blog at www.janeglenchur.blogspot.com.